THE SE

By

PHILLIP RICH

EKKLISIA PROPHETIC APOSTOLIC MINISTRIES, INC.

PUBLISHED BY EKKLISIA MINISTRIES, INC
Copyright 2007 A. D.

All rights reserved under International Copyright law. No part of this publication may be reproduced, stored in a retrieval system, or transmitted, in whole or in part, in any form or by any means, electronic, mechanical, photocopying, recording or otherwise, without the prior express consent of the publisher. All scripture is the Kings James Version unless otherwise stated. All rights reserved.

Take note that the name satan is not capitalized. We choose not to acknowledge him, even to the point of violating grammatical rules.

Table of Contents

The Assigned Word 1

Position Yourself to Receive 8

The Sent Word Becomes Flesh 27

The Sent Word Produces Faith 41

Send Now Prosperity 55

The Assigned Word

Psalms 107:20; *"He sent his word, and healed them, and delivered them from their destructions."*

"He sent his word" speaks of God sending His Word. It is the sent word that brought healing. Not just any word, <u>but</u> a *sent* word. *"Sent"* (Hebrew: *shalach, shaw-lakh'*) means the appointed or the assigned word. You will find that it is the appointed, the assigned word God gives us that brings the benefit. It is the sent word that brings the healing. It is the sent word that brings the deliverance. It is the sent word that brings the prosperity. It is the sent word that brings us out of where we have been into where we need to go. It is the sent word, the assigned word, the appointed word, the now word, the fresh word, the fresh *rhema*, the fresh manna that God has released for an appointed time for an appointed purpose that brings an appointed blessing.

That is the word that healed them and delivered them.

Isaiah 55:11; *"So shall <u>my</u> word be that goeth forth out of <u>my</u> mouth: it shall not return unto me void, but it shall accomplish that which I please, and it shall prosper in the thing whereto I <u>sent</u> it."*

In other words, God is saying that He is the one to send an appointed word, an assigned word. It is not just any word. It is not throwing the Bible open and finding a promise. That really won't do it. That is not an assigned word. That is not an appointed word because it is a *logos* word and not a *rhema* word. A *rhema* word is a **now** word with an appointment, as assignment that will not return void but will prosper in the thing wherein He has sent it. It will bring forth the desired result.

We can't separate God from His Word. Jesus Himself is called the Word. So you need to go to God and connect God with His Word. Don't try to pray outside of the Word of God. When you pray, take your Bible with you and let God begin to speak to you. Let God begin to get into this thing and make it alive to you.

The Sent Word will Prosper

The sent Word will prosper where He has sent it. If He hasn't sent it, it won't prosper. It won't work for you to get a little promise book and try to make something happen. However, there is nothing wrong with feeding on the promises of God until God sends a word. That is part of the feed and seed process. You have to feed and seed until God speaks an appointed, an assigned word.

Isaiah 9:8; *"The Lord sent a word into Jacob, and it hath lighted* [came to be known, came to pass] *upon Israel."*

That which is sent by God lights upon you and comes to pass. It becomes personal. That is the difference between having **the** word and having **a** word. When **the** word becomes **a** word, you have just received an assigned word. The assigned, appointed word is a word that will prosper in your life. That is a word that won't return to Him void. It will accomplish everything He pleases.

If you remember, the Old Testament prophets made statements like, *"The word of the Lord came unto me saying..."* before they would ever speak. They weren't repeating what some other prophet said, what some other preacher told them or what some other believer told them. They waited on God until the word of the Lord came to them. They waited for an assigned word, an appointed word. When the appointed word came they rose up, spoke and God performed it.

I used to wonder why the Bible said that God never let one of Samuel's words fall to the ground void, until I understood that Samuel only spoke what God made alive to his heart. He only spoke the assigned words, the appointed words. He didn't just speak a *logos* word. He didn't just speak what he heard someone else say. He didn't just say what was righteous or religious to say or what would make somebody happy. He spoke what God told him to say.

It is the assigned word that changes us. It is the assigned word that we need.

1 Kings 17:2; *"And the word of the LORD came unto him, saying,"*

Why does it say *came*? Because the Lord sent him a word. When you don't know what to do, you need God to send a word. When you are sick in body, you need God to send a word. When you are down and out, you need God to send a word. When there is trouble in your home, you need God to send a word. In whatever you are facing, you need a sent word, an appointed word, an assigned word. You are one assigned word away from a major victory and miracle. No matter what you are facing right now you are one sent word away from a total radical miracle change. Just one word will change your life.

1 Kings 17:3-6; *"Get thee hence, and turn thee eastward, and hide thyself by the brook Cherith, that is before Jordan. And it shall be, that thou shalt drink of the brook; and I have commanded the ravens to feed thee there. So he went and did according unto the word of the LORD: for he went and dwelt by the brook Cherith, that is before Jordan. And the ravens brought him bread and flesh in the morning, and bread and flesh in the evening; and he drank of the brook."*

Why was it that he was able to drink from the brook during a time when there was no water anywhere? Why was it that he was able to have food when there wasn't any? The reason is because of a sent word. The word of the Lord came, was sent to him. That sent word produced exactly what it was sent to do, provide for the prophet water, food, and sustenance. The very word that was sent produced the very sustenance that was needed.

When the situation changed a little bit, God was ready to send another word. If your season is changing and it looks like the brook is drying up, don't be afraid, don't get upset with God, or get fearful. God is getting ready to send another word. That sent word is going to make everything all right. You are just one sent word away from total blessing at all times. Man shall not live by bread alone but by every sent word that proceeds from the mouth of God. That is how we eat. That is how we breathe.

Get this into your spirit. What I am teaching is a sent word. This sent word will release a blessing into your life. It is going to prosper. It will not return void but will accomplish that which He pleases.

The brook dried up and that season of blessing had ended. When the season of blessing ends it doesn't mean that God wants you to do without. It means that He wants you to seek Him again for a sent word. God will never let us get comfortable with our faith. He always demands an increase of faith. He will never let your faith get lazy. In all the years that I have served Him, He has only tightened down and increased my faith. The treadmill is almost going full blast now. I am running to try and keep up with it. It started going real slow and I kind-of got used to it. Then it got a little faster and I got used to that. Then faster and now I am at a full run.

For each new level there is a sent word. There is an assigned word that brings success to that level. Whatever challenge you are facing, God wants you to seek Him for a sent word. There is a sent word that brings blessing into that situation. You can't live on yesterday's sent word, yesterday's manna. Manna that is more than a day old will breed worms and disease.[1] You can't live on yesterday's experiences, on yesterday's word. You can't live on yesterday's shout or dance. You have to have a **now** sent word. You need a **now** word for a **now** situation. We are told the Israelites went out every day for manna, for a sent word. It is the sent word that feeds you. It is the sent word that gives you sustenance. It gives you strength to serve the Lord, strength to rise up and defeat devils, to take back territory, to get your loved ones into the kingdom. You have to have a sent word.

We have been trying to eat old manna and get by with it. And we wonder why we don't have much strength. We need a sent word every day.

---

[1] Exodus 16:20

1 Kings 17:8-9; *"And the word of the LORD came unto him, saying, Arise, get thee to Zarephath, which belongeth to Zidon, and dwell there: behold, I have commanded a widow woman there to sustain thee."*

Elijah got another sent word that sustained him for almost two years. God knew His sent word would so affect somebody who had nothing, that they would have something to give to the man of God to sustain him during a season when there was nothing to have.

Sent words give you something where there is nothing. They give you something to give to others while there is nothing. Sent words contain the very power, life, and ability of God. They contain it and produce it. There is a supply source of God in them. You don't have to know how it is going to happen. You don't have to try and figure out which way God is going to do it, because about the time you have it figured out, He will turn around and bless you another way. I can't tell you how many times I said, *"I never expected it to come from that direction."* That is what the sent word will do. It will make somebody take care of you who doesn't like you and doesn't want to take care of you. The sent word will make somebody bless you who despises you and they will bless you more than they would bless somebody they love. The sent word changes things and makes things happen. It is such an awesome word that there is no way your mind can comprehend it. There is no way you can figure it out. There is no way you can put it together in the natural. That is the sent word.

The Sent Word Will Produce Miracles

The prophet Elijah knew that if God gave a sent word for him to go to a certain place there was miracle power in that sent word he could tap into and release into the situation. So when he went to the woman he tapped into the sent word. He spoke to her what God spoke and released the power of the sent word to the woman so that not only was the prophet cared for, but the woman and her son lived for many days.

1 Kings 17:16; *"And the barrel of meal wasted not* [of course it didn't, the sent word produced]*, neither did the cruse of oil fail* [of course not, the sent word was producing something]*, according to the* [sent] *word of the LORD, which he spake by Elijah."*

Notice, God sent the word but He expected a vessel to pass it on. When the sent word comes, particularly if He is sending it not only to us but to others, it can be passed on and the benefit will be released not only to you but also to those you love and come in contact with. *"The barrel of meal wasted not and neither did the cruse of oil fail according to the word of the Lord."* This was done according to the word God sent Elijah to speak. We also have to know when that sent word is just to us personally and when a sent word is also for our families, our friends or the people we are about to minister to.

In a later chapter we will talk about what we need to do to always receive the sent word, pick it up, hear what God is saying and be able to benefit from the sent word.

Jeremiah 29:11; *"For I know the thoughts that I think toward you, saith the LORD, thoughts of peace, and not of evil, to give you an expected end."*

God's thoughts toward you are of prosperity and blessing, to give you a future, a hope and an expected end. The sent word of God to you will come in line with the thoughts that He has toward you. When He gives you an assigned word, it is nothing less than blessed. It is the best.

God is sending words, giving forth fresh *rhema*, fresh manna, every day, but many people miss it. A lot of people are bound by religion, bound by not knowing what God's Word says. Hosea 4:6 says, *"My people are destroyed for lack of knowledge."* They have no revelation. They don't understand so they don't benefit from the sent word. They miss the sent word. They don't pick it up and receive it, so there is no benefit. But there is a sent word and God is sending it.

The Prophetic Word

A form of the sent word is the prophetic word for our lives and situations, although it doesn't carry the gravity of the Word of God in the sense of the written becoming the sent word.

I have noticed that if I speak to people what God is telling me to say to them, then that is what God produces in their life. If I am saying what I think they would like to hear, if I pump their flesh a little bit or if I soulishly give them what they want, then God doesn't back that because it is not a sent word. If I wait on the Holy Ghost until there is an unction to function and a sent word comes, then release that word into their lives, there is power to produce. God backs His Word. He backs the sent word.

I learned a long time ago that it does me no good to try to prophesy to everybody every night. If God is not giving me a specific word, why would I want to give a general? A general word is not a sent word. A good word is not the best word. The best is God speaking. The best is waiting for the unction, waiting for the impression, waiting for the speaking, waiting for the stirring, waiting for God to bring something up.

The word *"prophecy"* in the Old Testament means to bubble forth. That means it is coming from the Spirit of God within the spirit of the vessel. When it bubbles up it bubbles forth. It is not coming from your head, but from your spirit where the Spirit of the Lord is. It is what bubbles forth, bubbles up, that brings the change in the lives of people. If you want God to always back up what you say, then always say what He says. You want total success all the time then always say what He is giving you and only what He is giving you..

Do not try to initiate anything that is not first saturated in prayer. You cannot hear things if you do not pray because prayer makes you sensitive to hear God. The voice of God is so still and so small sometimes that we can overrun it with our flesh, our will, our thinking if we are not sensitized enough. The impressions can be so small that sometimes I think it is just me. If we haven't renewed our mind and put our carnal part down, our carnal self will take it away from us and we will never step out and speak it. Then we think we don't hear God.

Position Yourself to Receive

Meditation and contemplation will get us to the place of positioning ourselves to receive the sent word. This positioning we will call the seven secrets of supernatural service.

Meditation and Contemplation

The first secret is meditation and contemplation. You have to come to the place where you get a sent word because only the sent word bears fruit and we have to have that. A lot of people want to quickly grab a verse of scripture without meditating on it, contemplating or praying over it. They want to act on a *logos* word. Then they wonder why nothing happens. If you act on a raw *logos* word there are no results. You will become confused. You will think there is something wrong with you, God or His Word. The only thing wrong is that you don't understand how to get the power of the Word released in your life. You have to come to the place of feeding on the Word. I call it feed and seed. There are times when I will go into a feeding frenzy because I really have a need in a certain area. Example: healing because something has attacked my body. I will get all the scriptures I can on my need, feed and seed on them. I will read books on them, memorize scripture, and meditate on them until something comes alive on the inside of me. Then I stay on it. Feed and seed.

Psalms 1:1-3; *"Blessed is the man that walketh not in the counsel of the ungodly, nor standeth in the way of sinners, nor sitteth in the seat of the scornful. But his delight is in the law of the LORD; and in his law doth he meditate* [to go over and over something, to ponder on it in order to apply it to your life] *day and night. And he shall be like a tree planted by the rivers of water* [sounds like there is a revival going on]*, that bringeth* *forth his fruit in his season* [being fruitful]; *his leaf also shall not wither; and whatsoever he doeth shall prosper."*

The doing is connected to the meditating. We will be doing what we are meditating and it will work. We will not have any dry or down times if we have done the feed and seed adequately. You have to do it to a high enough level. I find it may take 3 or 4 days or even a week of feeding and seeding.

I remember one time I was out of revivals. I had several scheduled but they all cancelled. The Lord had shut me down for a season. All of my planned meetings had scheduling conflicts involving other ministries – sounds like a God thing. I didn't understand it but I knew I had to press into God. It came up in my spirit that His Word would take me through. I had been faithful in tithes and offerings, had been obeying the voice of the Lord. I had been making vows and paying them so I wasn't out on that part of it.

I have found that when it comes to prosperity, giving is a big part of the equation but it is not the only part of it. The Word is one of the biggest ingredients. You have to have a sent word about prosperity before you really prosper. You have to connect that Word with your obedience in giving. 3 John says, *"Beloved, I wish above all things that thou mayest prosper and be in health, even as thy soul prospereth."* Prosperity is connected with knowledge of the Word. You really can't prosper or walk in health without enough of the Word becoming a sent word, becoming a *rhema*, a manna to you.

So I began to seek the Lord. I started to feed and seed on every scripture I could find about prosperity, reading them over and over, studying them, and writing them down. For about a week I went over them as often as I could. At the end of the week while I was praying in the spirit, thinking and meditating on the scriptures I got quiet before the Lord. Out of my spirit came *"daily He loadeth us down with benefits"*.[2] The sent word had come. I let it roll over and over in my mind and in my spirit. I knew what daily meant – every day. Every day He loads me down, piles me up with benefits. I knew what benefits meant. Finances,

---

[2] Psalms 68:19

abundance are part of those benefits. Throughout the next few days I took the sent word, kept speaking it and meditating on it.

Once you hear, you start seeing in the realm of the spirit. What you see, you be. Once you perceive it you are able to receive it.

There is another verse in 1 Samuel 3 which talks about the word of the Lord being precious and there not being an open vision. The word *"precious"* means scarce. There wasn't much word and because of that there was no open vision. Without a vision people perish. But if you have a vision, you no longer perish. You can't see into the realm of the spirit until you have first heard God.

So I started seeing, in a vision, people knocking on my door everyday. They were ringing my doorbell handing me money and checks. Right after I had this vision, which was based on the *rhema*, my wife asked me what we were going to do about finances. I told her I had heard God and it was going to be all right. I shared with her the sent word and the vision I had. She said that would be wonderful because it had never happened before. Three days later what I had seen in the vision started happening. For three months, every week between $700-800 was handed to me. I did not pick up the phone and call anybody telling them I was low on funds. All I did was take it to God. Are you beginning to see that the sent word prospered me? When that season was over people quit coming to the door. Revivals opened up again.

God knows how to take care of you. Along with obedience in giving, you really can't prosper until you have a sent word. You have to feed and seed.

There are people who have given in abundance but have not seen the prosperity flowing because part of the equation is missing. Giving is a big part of it. When you make a cake, flour is a big part of it. But if you just have flour you don't have much of a cake. There are some other ingredients that may be insignificant by themselves but when you add them to the flour you get a cake. You have to have something to hold it all together with.

Proverbs 6:20-21; *"My son, keep thy father's commandment, and forsake not the law of thy mother: Bind them continually upon thine heart, and tie them about thy neck."*

"Thy father's commandment" and *"the law of thy mother"* are the Word. When you bind them continually upon your heart you are taking God's Word to your heart. That means you have to be reading the Word, meditating on the Word, feeding and seeding the Word, particularly in areas of your life that are lacking. If you need more finances, you need to do more feeding and seeding, more prayerful meditation on prosperity scriptures. If it is a physical problem, you need to feed and seed on the scriptures on healing until something begins to come forth. It is the same way with lost loved ones. You need to feed and seed on household salvation. There are answers that you can get at any time.

Proverbs 6:22; *"When thou goest, it shall lead thee* [You get enough of God's Word in you and you will get some leadership]*; when thou sleepest, it shall keep thee* [that is protection]*; and when thou awakest, it* [that is, the sent word, the *rhema* word] *shall talk with thee."*

You get a sent word when you bind the Word to your heart. You will get leadership when you don't know what to do. The Word of God will talk to you, speak to you. If you want to hear God, bind the Word in your heart until God makes it come alive and He talks to you right out of the Word you have been feeding on. There have been times when I have been through things and in the middle of the night exactly what I need comes up from my spirit. But I had to first feed and seed.

Fasting

Another secret is fasting. The Lord spoke to me that it is fasting *as directed*. We should be ready to do some form of fasting as the Holy Spirit directs us. There is more than one way to do it. I have had the Spirit of God tell me to do a Daniel fast where He told me what to eat and what not to eat. One time I fasted dark colas and chocolate for a couple of months. I did it until He released me from it. God blessed it because He didn't want me having them for that particular time. That is fasting as directed.

Matthew 6:16 says *when* you fast not *if* you fast. *When* gives us some understanding that we ought to be doing it sometime. Fasting should be a part of our life. If you are led by the Spirit, He will lead you into some form of fasting. Everybody can fast, even diabetics, because the Spirit of God will tell you how. Being led by the Holy Spirit is the most important thing of all.

Isaiah 58:6; *"Is not this the fast that I have chosen? to loose the bands of wickedness, to undo the heavy burdens, and to let the oppressed go free, and that ye break every yoke?"*

This scripture tells me that God chooses fasting. He chooses when you fast, how long the fast is going to be, what you eat and what you don't eat.

In one revival I was going into I sensed that I needed to fast because something had to be broken in the spirit realm. I asked the Lord what He wanted me to do. The impression came up in my spirit to do juice and water. They were to be alternated. I kept asking, listening and it came to me to start with 8 ounces of water and to pray beginning at 8 every morning. I was to rest in the afternoon until it was time for service. I could do that.

It came as an impression. When the Spirit of God speaks it is not always boomings. There is a light, gentle knowing inside your spirit all in line with the Word of God. I knew 8 ounces water at 8 am, 8 ounces juice at 9 am. He even gave me the impression as to what kind of juice. I was to alternate the water and juice every hour all through the day. I did that for 3 or 4 days.

We had an awesome breakthrough in the House of the Lord. God was moving in that place. It was the fast He chose. There have been times when He has told me to eat one meal a day. He let me know what to eat and I did it. There have been times He has said to fast one day and eat the next one. Some times He might tell me He only wants me to have vegetables and fruit for a few days. I may have to cut the sweets out for a while. I do it. It may be a television fast. Whatever He speaks for you to do, it is fasting when you obey what He is telling you to do, when you abstain from what He is telling you to. Every time I have obeyed what He has spoken to my heart I have seen results. That is what I am after. I am after results. I am after what works.

Isaiah 58:6; *"Is not this the fast that I have chosen? to loose the bands of wickedness, to undo the heavy burdens, and to let the oppressed go free, and that ye break every yoke?"*

Isaiah 58:9; *"Then shalt thou call, and the LORD shall answer* [This is talking about sent words. When I pray and ask Him to talk to me about things then out of His Word He is going to speak to me.]*; thou shalt cry, and he shall say, Here I am. If thou take away from the midst of thee the yoke, the putting forth of the finger, and speaking vanity;"*

The rest of Isaiah 58 goes on to talk more about fasting.

The part I want to emphasize is that God will begin to answer. The number one way He will do it is through His Word. If He answers through his Word, the answer that comes is the sent word that has power in it. It is the *rhema*, the *dabar*.

We really cannot get revelation without some form of fasting. It is a part of the equation. There have to be seasons, times of fasting. For me I have to do it quite often, because of doing revivals and ministering. I am not necessarily fasting every day or every week. When I go home, I don't fast. I eat with my wife and kids, play around and have fun because I am on the road a lot. But if you are home all the time then you can go ahead and fast. Just let the family know ahead of time what is going on.

I will tell you one thing about fasting – you need the grace to do it. So, if you know God is telling you to fast then He will give you the grace to do it.

Prayer in Tongues

The next secret is prayer in tongues. I pray a lot in the spirit and I believe that the more I pray in the Holy Ghost the more I am positioning myself to receive sent words. I build my spirit up, edify my spirit for a release of power to get divine secrets. Many of the divine secrets are simply revelations of the Word.

I have found that without a lot of prayer in the spirit, I don't get a lot of revelation. I don't get the revelation of the Word and I don't see revelation gifts working very much. The word of knowledge, word of wisdom and discerning of spirits become very dull in my spirit if I don't pray enough in tongues.

1 Corinthians 14:2; *"For he that speaketh in an unknown tongue speaketh not unto men, but unto God: for no man understandeth him; howbeit in the spirit he speaketh mysteries* [unknown things]*."*

I believe when we are praying in tongues many times we are positioning ourselves to get revelation on the Word, to unlock mysteries of revelation on the Word of God. If we could get a revelation on things that we don't understand, we could get a miracle. We are beginning to come to the place of speaking these divine mysteries so that later we will get what we call the bubble up effect. The word *prophecy* in the Old Testament means to bubble up in order to bubble forth. Some of us have not been doing enough bubbling up. If you will pray in the Holy Ghost you will build yourself up, you will edify yourself.[3]

1 Corinthians 14:4; *"He that speaketh in an unknown tongue edifieth himself;"*

He builds up his own spirit. The Word of God also builds up your spirit. I find that if I do a lot of praying in the Holy Spirit the Word of God just explodes to me. Smith Wigglesworth said that some read the Bible in the Hebrew, some read the Bible in the Greek, but he read the Bible in the Holy Ghost.

1 Corinthians 14:14-15; *"For if I pray in an unknown tongue, my spirit prayeth, but my understanding is unfruitful* [my mind doesn't know what I am saying]*. What is it then? I will pray with the spirit, and I will pray with the understanding also: I will sing with the spirit, and I will sing with the understanding also."*

---

[3] Jude 20

It doesn't take your mind to pray in tongues, it takes your spirit. That is why you can do other things while you are praying in tongues.

For a time I worked in an assembly plant that made oil seals for cars and trucks. I worked a press where I had to put 120 pieces of metal and rubber together in a tray, put the tray in a press and remove them when the time was up. While one tray was in the press I was loading the next one. It was noisy there so I would pray in tongues or even sing in tongues while I loaded the trays. It didn't hinder me. In fact, I put out more quality parts. It doesn't take your head to pray in tongues. If it takes your head, you are not praying in tongues. You have something else going on.

Paul is saying that his spirit was praying and his head did not understand. You can sing in the spirit and also sing with the understanding. You can pray in tongues and pray in the vernacular. Many times, if you know how to yield, you can actually be praying the interpretation of what you prayed in tongues. Oral Roberts did and that is where Oral Roberts University came from. Everything he has ever done in the ministry came from praying in tongues.

The more that you yield to praying in the spirit the more you can pray in the spirit and the more you can switch into different languages as God leads you. You can even go into divers tongues. There are depths we have not probed yet. There are places we have never gone yet in the spirit but we can and it will benefit us in reaching the world for Jesus. Becoming more like Christ will benefit us in our lives. I have found out that I can read the Word and pray in tongues at the same time. When I do, it comes alive and jumps off the page at me. The more I do it the quicker I get revelation out of the Word.

This is something the Holy Spirit wants us to know because it will cause sent words to be released to us. Sent words have the power in them to be released to do what they say.

So much of this takes time to explain, but when you do it, it happens in a split second. How many have had the Holy Spirit download revelation into your spirit, but it takes forever to try and tell someone about it? I remember one night when the heavens opened and the Lord showed me some stuff about the coming glory and what is going to be happening. He downloaded, with the computer of heaven, so much tremendous information in a split second that it would take me hours or even days to try and explain to you. I am not sure I am aware of what all is there. That is how awesome our God is.

Inquiring and Listening

If you want a sent word, inquire and listen. You must come into *koinonia* with the Spirit of God.

2 Corinthians 13:14; *"The grace of the Lord Jesus Christ, and the love of God, and the communion of the Holy Ghost, be with you all. Amen."*

"Communion" is *koinonia* which means intimacy, communication, partnership, both of you carrying a load together, both coming together over a common interest and together working together to bring it about. It is more than communication. It is intimate communication for the same purpose. You both have the same interest. You both want the same thing to happen.

The Holy Spirit has an interest. His interest is to build you up, for you to mature, be a soul winner and build up somebody else. When your interest is that same thing then you can come into *koinonia* with the Him. The Holy Spirit will talk to you, speak to you. You can ask Him questions and He will answer them. I ask the Holy Spirit to explain what He is trying to tell me and when I get quiet and listen, the answer bubbles up, the scripture bubbles up. It is so sweet and matter of fact. That is the way it is supposed to be. If you are cold, dead and dry in your spirit, you can ask questions and hear nothing. You wouldn't recognize Him if He spoke to you or hit you in the head with something. You can't be dead spiritually and have any of this work. Something has to be kept constant and alive. It is a relationship much like a marriage. You have to keep it flowing. You have to work on the relationship. You have to say some sweet things along the way. You have to plant some good seeds of love along the way.

If I want sweet things from my wife I will start saying the nicest things. I may start saying them a week in advance. Once in a while I do flowers. I might write a note or a card. What am I doing? I am working on a relationship. When you work on it a lot then it will, all of a sudden, open a greater intimacy of communication. That is *koinonia*.

Did you know that you have to woo the Holy Ghost if you want Him to talk to you? Don't just expect Him to open up and throw everything your way. You have to understand that there is a relationship where the Spirit of God is a lover to you. You have to woo Him.

You can't read the Song of Solomon without understanding what I am talking about. It tells us about spiritual, not physical, intimacy with the Lord. It is about Christ and the church, about an intimate relationship with God. When we begin to develop that relationship, there will be a drawing of our spirit. *"Come away my beloved."* You will be wooing Him and you will feel Him wooing you back. You will hear His voice and the line of communication will be open. The little knowings down inside, the impressions will start flowing. It is there. You ask a question and the answer comes. Sometimes it comes as quickly as you ask. The sent word.

Revelation 3:20; *"Behold, I stand at the door, and knock: if any man hear my voice, and open the door, I will come in to him, and will sup with him, and he with me."*

Several years ago while I was at Oral Roberts University the Lord did this in my life. I was in graduate school and was busy. I had myself so loaded down with stuff that I wasn't praying very much. I wasn't reading the Word very much. One morning at 6 a.m., right before the time I was to get up, I heard a knocking at my door. I was living in the graduate housing at that time. Not fully awake, I shook myself and began to listen. I didn't hear it again so I laid back down and started to doze again. Then I heard the knocking once more. I sat up, listened and again didn't hear anything. In a little bit it started again. This time I got up and checked the front door. No one was there. I started walking back to bed and I heard the Holy Spirit say, *"Behold, I stand at the door, and knock: if any man hear my voice, and open the door, I will come in to him, and will sup with him, and he with me."* This was not written to the world but to the seven churches of Asia Minor, the church of Laodicea in particular. This is the church we are in today.

He began to tell me what it meant. He said, *"My people are not coming into koinonia with me. Knocking on the door means I want them to open a door of opportunity to have communion, intimacy with me. I am knocking which means I am wooing."*

All of a sudden you may feel like you need to pray. That is the knock. All of a sudden you may feel like you need to read the Word more. That is the knock. But do you do it? He said, *"If any man will hear my voice and open the door of opportunity I will come in to him and sup with him."* Sup means *koinonia*, intimate relationship. We are going to eat the Word of God at this supper, this communion. He will break bread with us. We can ask questions and He will reveal it to us. That is the sent word, which produces. When you lack understanding of the Word you lack the power that is behind that Word.

In the parable of the sower[4] what caused the soils to be bad and not produce anything was that they didn't understand the Word of God. The soil that produces is the soil of the heart that understands the Word and then brings forth fruit. Without understanding you don't bring forth fruit, don't know how to do the Word of God. The word understanding is connected to the word revelation, which means a sent word. You and I are desperate for God to bring forth the revelation of the Word to us. We are just one revelation away from any miracle we need. Revelation and understanding are the same term. It is important for us to catch this.

Probing and Monitoring

Now, let's look at probing and monitoring the realm of the spirit and doing it by the Spirit of God, by the ability of God.

A lot of people go by what is seen.

2 Corinthians 4:18; *"While we look not at the things which are seen, but at the things which are not seen: for the things which are seen are temporal* [or changeable, can't be relied upon]*; but the things which are not seen are eternal* [without change and can be totally relied upon]*."*

---

[4] Matthew 13, Luke 8 and Mark 4

We have to get to the place where we see the unseen, where we look with our spiritual eyes and quit relying so much on what we see with our natural eyes. The Word of God is so clear on some things. Jesus spoke about those people who have eyes to see but they see not.

1 Corinthians 15:44 speaks of a natural man and a spiritual man. Your natural man has five senses which enable it to function in the natural. Your spirit man has five senses which enable it to function in the spirit realm. We have majored on the natural realm and have not really focused our spiritual eyes or used our spiritual senses very much. Paul said it is time we quit just looking with the natural, but start checking things out with our spiritual senses. Things are not always as they appear.

I was trained under a man of God who, when he was nineteen years old, would press into the spirit and probe the things of the spirit. He did this while working for an insurance company. When it came time to sell insurance to people, he would get into the spirit. The Spirit of the Lord would show him the hearts of people, show him the situations, show him who would be a good risk and who would be a bad risk, who he was wasting his time on and who would be a good person to spend time on. That is how he operated in his sales. At nineteen he became a millionaire and the top salesman of the insurance company. He did it by not looking at the things that are seen but the things that are not seen.

Behind my natural eyes are spiritual eyes that can see in the realm of the spirit. Behind my natural ears are spiritual ears that can hear in the realm of the spirit. There are times when my spiritual nose has been able to smell things. There are times when I can smell demons. They stink. Jesus called them foul spirits because they smell bad. They each have a distinct smell that you can't smell with your natural nose. You smell it with your spiritual nose.

Your spirit man is called the inner man or the hidden man of the heart and is more real than your physical man. Your spirit man also has feelings. Don't go by natural feelings but by spiritual feelings. All of a sudden in the spiritual realm there is uneasiness. A caution light comes on. It is time to get into the area of probing and monitoring.

Proverbs 20:27; *"The spirit of man is the candle of the LORD, searching all the inward parts of the belly."*

This verse says that my spirit man has the ability to probe the depths of the spirit and tell me what is really truth and what is a lie. I have been around some people and the Spirit of God would let me know that everything they were telling me was a lie. There have been other times when I have been around people and the Holy Ghost has told me they are real even if others said they weren't.

Years ago there was a ministry the Holy Ghost connected me with that everyone else said was off the wall. He was this and that. But in my spirit, the Holy Ghost told me he was real and that He would prove it to me. One night I was attending a large crusade in Tulsa. I told the Lord that even though He told me the man was real, I wanted a little more proof. God said okay. He told me that He would show me fourteen people this man would minister to before he got to them. A little later I saw a light over a couple sitting on the front row before he walked over to them and began to minister to them. The bright light shifted to another area and he walked over there and began to minister to the people there. It happened just like that for fourteen people. I said, *"Okay that is you, Lord."* Later the Holy Ghost began to give me information about words of knowledge before this man said it to people.

The Holy Ghost will do that for us, but we have to get ourselves to that place. We have to position our spirits. We have to quit operating so much in the flesh, in the natural. It is hindering us. If the church would ever get out of the flesh and get into the spirit we could win the world for Jesus Christ. I believe we are heading that way. There are people who want to be what God destined them to be.

Find the Grove

The next secret is finding the grove and getting in it.

Flow in the spirit and operate there. Usually there is a key to get in the grove and to stay there, to stay in the niche, in the flow of the Spirit of God. There is a key that brings total success to that situation. There is a key that every church needs. By getting into the grove, the key that will unlock the very growth of that church can be found. Every ministry has to get into the grove and get the key. There is a key for the success of every ministry.

There is a key that makes marriages successful. There is a key that causes children to want to be saved and serve the Lord. There is a key to every relationship. There is a key for every ministry. There is a key for every church. There is a key to every situation. No matter what it is, no matter what you face there is a key. You have to get into the spirit and find it. When you get it, begin to use it. It is called *keys of the kingdom*.

Revelation 1:10; *"I was in the Spirit on the Lord's day, and heard behind me a great voice, as of a trumpet,"*

John said he was in the spirit on the Lord's Day and heard a voice. Then he began to see Jesus. Jesus is the key to everything. He has all the keys. What we must know is that it is in the spirit where we begin to see and hear. We begin to see Jesus and He is the one with the keys.

You have to get in the spirit, which means you have to ignore the natural. You have to ignore your flesh, your body. What I mean is that the body out of control is flesh and flesh is sin. You control your body, put it in check. In the New Testament the word *"body"* means slave. Your body is your slave, not your master. When your body becomes your master, it has transformed to flesh.

Flesh, when it has conceived, leads to death. The body out of control is sin and sin leads to death. The way we get into the spirit is by controlling our natural body and making it the slave God meant it to be. Your body should be a slave to your spirit and to your soul. You are to be spirit-led with your soul mastering over your body, keeping it in check so that it doesn't enter into flesh. That way you won't be a carnal Christian, flesh ruled, body ruled.

In the natural John was not in a place where he could accommodate his body at all. On the isle of Patmos there was no good, fresh water. There was intense heat during the day and intense cold at night. There was no food to eat. The Romans put him there to kill him. They expected him to die.

There was no place of comfort, yet he said he was in the spirit on the Lord's Day. We think we can't get into the spirit unless there is a soft chair with air conditioning or heat. But getting into the spirit goes far beyond the natural. People have accommodated their bodies so much that they have become flesh ruled Christians and that is why there have not been many revivals in the churches. There has been too much carnality. Paul said that is what causes divisions and fights in the church. "*I don't like that preacher and if you do, then I am breaking it off with you.*" Carnality causes division.

Revelation 1:10; *"I was in the Spirit on the Lord's day, and heard behind me a great voice, as of a trumpet,"*

While you are in the spirit you can hear God. To be in the spirit means to mind the things of the spirit, to press into the spirit, to focus on the things of the Spirit of God. Where is your focus? It will tell you what you are doing. If you are focusing on the natural, on *me, me, me* you are all flesh, which means you are entering into sin. But if your focus is God, serving Him, and wanting to please Him you are in the spirit while you are doing that. Where you focus is the direction you will head. If you are focusing on getting your own needs met, focusing on your own life you will pay attention to flesh. Being in the spirit means focusing on the things of God and putting our priorities on Him.

Revelation 1:10-12; *"I was in the Spirit on the Lord's day, and heard behind me a great voice, as of a trumpet, Saying, I am Alpha and Omega, the first and the last: and, What thou seest, write in a book, and send it unto the seven churches which are in Asia; unto Ephesus, and unto Smyrna, and unto Pergamos, and unto Thyatira, and unto Sardis, and unto Philadelphia, and unto Laodicea. And I turned to see the voice that spake with me. And being turned, I saw seven golden candlesticks;"*

When he began to focus on what he had heard, John began to see. The seven golden candlesticks mean seven revelations. A candlestick represents light, revelation and so verse 12 begins with a seven-fold revelation of Jesus, which corresponds to the seven golden candlesticks.

Revelation 1:13-16; *"And in the midst of the seven candlesticks one like unto the Son of man, clothed with a garment* [robes of righteousness] *down to the foot, and girt about the paps with a golden girdle. His head and his hairs were white like wool, as white as snow; and his eyes were as a flame of fire; And his feet* [churches that witness] *like unto fine brass, as if they burned in a furnace; and his voice* [the prophetic] *as the sound of many waters. And he had in his right hand seven stars: and out of his mouth went a sharp twoedged sword: and his countenance was as the sun shineth in his strength."*

It goes on to talk about the seven churches. Each church had a different revelation of Jesus. We need all of them and that is why we shouldn't speak against other churches and feel like we are the only one who can do anything. We need the seven revelations of Jesus.

Revelation 1:17-18; *"And when I saw him, I fell at his feet as dead. And he laid his right hand upon me, saying unto me, Fear not; I am the first and the last: I am he that liveth, and was dead; and, behold, I am alive for evermore, Amen; and <u>have the keys</u> of hell and of death."*

There is a key that will unlock your situation. There is a key to everything in the spirit, but you can't use somebody else's key. Years ago, a man named Tommy Barnett held church growth seminars for the denomination I was in at the time. We all went to the seminars to learn everything we could because God had given him a key while he was in the spirit. The key was to use buses to bring people to church. He had great success using that key. Everyone else wanted that success and began to use that key. They bought a fleet of buses, but it didn't work because every town has a key to unlock the town. You have to get a special key for each situation. You can't use somebody else's key.

You need a healing? Don't just listen to how someone else got healed. No, you have to get your own key. God has one just for you to take care of your situation and get you what you need in God. You have to get into the spirit where Jesus is because He has a key for you.

God is opening some things up. We have to move on into the spirit. We have to step out of carnality and flesh. We have to start controlling our bodies, limiting our bodies, giving our bodies what they need. Scripture says a man will nourish and cherish his body. He is supposed to do that. But never accommodate its every whim because at that point you enter flesh and flesh is sin which leads to death. So you balance and limit your flesh. Control your flesh like you control a little child. It doesn't know what it should eat. It doesn't know when it should go to bed. It doesn't know its limitations. You have to rise up with the Spirit of God in your spirit and with your soul, set order, and give your body orders. Our physical bodies are spoiled and they don't know what is good for them. They will eat too much, sleep too much, get too much entertainment, and too much rest.

Remember, the body out of control is flesh and flesh is sin. Romans 8 says that when we are in the flesh we cannot please God. You cannot be led by the Spirit of God and be led by your flesh. If you want to hear God you have to deal with flesh. If you want a sent word you have to deal with flesh. That means we go to church when we know we are supposed to and we tell our bodies that we are going. We give tithes and offerings not because our body wants to do it, but because the Word tells us to do it. Every once in a while, just to keep my body in order, I will tell my body it cannot have that extra piece of pie no matter how badly it wants it. It isn't going to get that extra hour of sleep either, even if it whines and cries about it. I am going to get up and pray. Who is the master?

The word *"body"* means slave, it is not to be the master over you. If we can learn this we are talking about real spirituality. We are talking about being able to walk in the power of the Spirit of God, be in the spirit on the Lord's Day and be able to hear, see and get the keys.

God is Everything

Another thing that brings us to where the Lord can do something awesome in our behalf is coming to understand that God is everything to us. We have to come to the place where nothing means more to us than God. Your job doesn't mean more to you than God. Your finances don't mean more to you than anything in God. It is not just a word that you are speaking, but you prove it.

Do you know why God wants the first ten percent? It is because He wants you to put Him first. He wants you to trust Him first. It is a part of being spiritual. People who cannot give tithes and offerings have not crossed over to being spiritual. They are still carnal because they can't trust God. They still want to trust the arm of the flesh. You have to get to the place where you believe God and are going to do what God's Word says above everything.

I have been around miracle ministries all of my life. I have been with ministries that have raised the dead and gotten people out of wheelchairs on a regular basis. Tumors and growths fell off of people, blind eyes would see, deaf ears would open, all kinds of miracles would happen. There were creative miracles of all kinds. They raised eight or nine people from the dead. Some were people whom the doctors had already done death certificates for.

The Spirit of the Lord would come on one ministry and people would be raised from the dead. You cannot do that and live in the flesh because a carnal person cannot raise anyone from the dead. This particular minister was one of the greatest givers I have ever met in my life, as liberal as anyone I have ever met. I have seen times when everything that came in a crusade was given to another ministry where it was needed to pay bills. He gave because the voice of God was there. This man was my pastor.

I was at a meeting where he had spent $5,000 on television advertising to promote the meeting. The offering came to $5,000. The Lord spoke to my pastor and told him to give the money to the local pastor. He reminded the Lord that he would be $5,000 in debt for the meeting if he did that because of the advertising bills. A carnal man would have had problems with giving that. But following the voice of God, he took the check, went to the pastor's office, knocked on the door and walked in. The pastor had been praying. His hands were on his face and he was leaning over on his desk. My pastor laid the check in front of him. This pastor asked what he was doing and my pastor told him that God had spoken to give him the check. That pastor told him he had just received a phone call telling him that the balloon payment on their building was due that day. He had to pay it the next morning or they would lose their building. The amount due was $5,000. That kind of giving is what enabled him to raise the dead.

I heard one minister say that through our obedience in giving we build our faith to the level of being able to raise the dead. Get a hold of this and you will gladly invest heavily into ministries, particularly the ones who are teaching and preaching the truth to you and the ones who are anointed because you will understand what is happening here. Not only is the Gospel being furthered by your giving, but you are being developed by your giving into a greater level of faith.

Luke 16:10-11; *"He that is faithful in that which is least is faithful also in much: and he that is unjust in the least is unjust also in much. If therefore ye have not been faithful in the unrighteous mammon, who will commit to your trust the true riches?"*

In other words, if you can't be faithful in your giving God is not going to give you the riches of the Spirit. He is not going to give you power to raise the dead if you cannot give tithes and offerings because He can't trust you with it. He will test you to see whether or not you can handle the greater power. If you can handle finances then God knows you can handle the power of God. If you can't overcome the flesh and God starts using you in a powerful way, you will wind up merchandising. You have to become selfless and get rid of the selfish. One way to do that is through giving. You get rid of covetousness by giving.

The Sent Word Becomes Flesh

Psalms 107:20; *"He sent his word, and healed them, and delivered them from their destructions."*

The sent word is the appointed word for a particular situation. God has an appointed word for an appointed time for an appointed need. So, whatever your need is, you need a special appointed word from God for that particular need. You can't live off of someone else's word for their situation. It won't work for you.

God has an appointed word for every need and it may be a little different than what someone else might receive. I have seen people try to live off of someone else's appointed word and not get the desired results. You have to get a special appointed word for you. You have to receive it. There is one special word just for you that will fit every problem, every situation, and every difficulty. For every place in your life where you need a miracle there is an appointed word that God will give you if you will seek Him for it.

Isaiah 55:11; *"So shall my word be that goeth forth out of my mouth: it shall not return unto me void, but it shall accomplish that which I please, and it shall prosper in the thing whereto I sent it."*

The sent word is a fresh word out of God's mouth for our situation. It is spoken by the Holy Ghost to us in our situation and will not return void. It will accomplish that which He pleases and will prosper. It is going to happen, going to bear fruit. The desired results will be there when we get the sent word.

We are learning how to acquire the sent word. No matter what problem we are facing we can get the sent word. It is going to prosper in the thing to which He has sent it.

Many will open their Bible and get a *logos* word. But a *logos* word doesn't have the release of power. The power is in it, but the release isn't there. People want to quickly grab a verse out of the Bible and make something happen. But it is the Word that comes fresh out of His mouth, the sent word that will do it. We have to understand the principles of God in order to see the power of God released. People have tried to work the Bible. No, no, no. You have to get into the Spirit with God. God and His Word cannot be separated. You need the Spirit of God connected with the Word of God, the Word and the Spirit in agreement. 1 John 5:7 says that the Word and the Spirit are one and they agree. We need to understand that it takes the Spirit and the Word together in order to see the desired result.

Spirit and Word

Some people are just trying to take the Word by itself. But it is dry and there is no release of power. It is like taking a seed, throwing it into dry ground and expecting something to happen. Without the water there is no germination and no release of what is in the seed. Sure, there is potential power in the seed but there is no release without the water. The Holy Ghost is likened unto the water. You have to have the water connected with the seed and then you have germination. You have a release of the power that is in the seed. The sent word does that. The sent word is the Spirit releasing the power that is locked up within the seed of the *logos* word. When it becomes the *rhema* word it becomes a sent word that will not return void.

Confession is a good thing, but outside of the Holy Ghost it becomes works. If you and I just confess one thousand scriptures to try to get something to happen, we are involved in works. The works of the flesh will never bring about the desired works of the spirit. But if you connect with the Spirit of God, seek Him for a fresh word you are talking about the power that is within the word coming to pass in your life. God chooses the verse you need.

In the last chapter we talked about feed and seed. You have to feed and seed on the written word of God. You have to feed and seed on good teaching of the Word of God. You need to feed and seed on that and then prayerfully take it to the Lord. The Lord will bring forth something out of that word on which you have been meditating. This is very important. We cannot take the Word without taking God. The Word is Jesus, but there is also the Holy Ghost and the Father. We need all three.

If the Holy Ghost had not come down and descended on Jesus, His ministry would not have done anything. Yet, Jesus is the Word. He was baptized by John the Baptist and consecrated Himself so the Holy Ghost could come down upon Him. He was full of the Holy Ghost and driven by the Spirit into the wilderness to be tempted by the devil for forty days and forty nights. He came out of that with great power and with great anointing. The Word took on the release of power after the Holy Ghost came upon Him.

Are you beginning to see that it takes the Spirit and the Word to have the power of God? Not just one or the other, but both of them together. That is why it is not enough for us to pray all the time. We have to get the Word in there with it. It is not enough just to have the Word all the time and no prayer because you are not putting the Holy Ghost into it. The equation has to have all the variables in order for it to work right.

I heard one minister say that all prayer puffs you up while all Word dries you up. Put the two together and it grows you up. It is not all one or all the other. Couple them together. That is how it works. It is the Spirit and the Word. There is total agreement. There is total release of potential power. The Word has potential power, but the catalyst of the Spirit of God releases the potential that is in the Word. We all know that there is potential power in the Word of God and the way you unlock that potential is through the Spirit of the Lord. That is why we need a move of God along with our study of the Word, along with our meditation on the Word of God. Thank God for the river of God, but if all you have is a river you have no fruit still. A revelation of the Word has to come forth out of it. There has to be a marriage of the two, a coupling of the two. You have to put the Word together with the Spirit of God and prayer is what brings the move of the Spirit. You have to have prayer coupled with meditation and the feeding and seeding of the Word. The moment they come together there is a tremendous releasing of power. God is beginning to show us these things through His Word so that we can enter the greater things of God.

Jesus was a man of prayer even though He was also the living Word.

John 1:14; *"And the Word was made flesh, and dwelt among us, (and we beheld his glory, the glory as of the only begotten of the Father,) full of grace and truth."*

He, Jesus, was the Word that became flesh. It is so important for us to understand it. Do you know how the Word became flesh? Mary asked the angel how it was going to happen. She asked how the Word could become flesh. The angel answered her, " *By the Holy Ghost."* Do you know how the Word is going to become flesh in your life? By the Holy Ghost. Are you ready for the Word to become flesh in your life? Are you ready for those scriptures about prosperity to become flesh? Are you ready for those scriptures about healing to become flesh? Are you catching where I am going with this? You wonder how this is going to happen? By the Holy Ghost. How is the Word going to become flesh in our lives? When I say, *"become flesh,"* I am asking, *"How is the Word going to become manifest?"* By the Holy Ghost.

The Manifested Word

When you understand these principles you can always see manifestations of the Word in your life. You can always get it. That means you can always get your prosperity. You can always get your healing. You can always receive the things that you desire from God because you will know what to do. You will know how to position yourself. It won't be a work of the flesh if you know how to position yourself.

The woman with the issue of blood knew all she had to do was position herself.[5] She said, *"If I can just touch the hem of His garment. If I can just get to where He is and touch Him then I know I shall be made whole."* She knew she had to position herself. Just the act of getting there

---

[5] Mark 5:25-34

wouldn't do anything. She knew that wherever Jesus was, wherever His power was, wherever His spirit was, wherever His walk was she had to position herself near Him. Get near Him. Get to Him.

Everything we read in the Bible is about a relationship with God. It is a manual to connect us to God. There is power in the manual itself, but it is in the meaning of it that the power lay. It is not the paper or the ink or the leather around it. There are religious people who are worshipping paper and ink and leather. They worship it so much that they dare not even touch it to read it. They lay it next to their beds at night thinking that somehow the holiness of the paper and ink will, by osmosis, flow over into their brains and their lives. They think that the paper and the ink are the power. It is not the paper and the ink, but the revelation that they need. It is the meaning. It is like getting love letters from somebody and so connecting with the love letters that when the writer shows up you ignore the writer and continue to hang on the love letters.

There will be a time in heaven when we will have the living Word before us. This book will never be discarded but we won't have it like we have it now. We will have Him. Once the lover of your life is there you won't need the paper and the ink because you have the person.

We need a sent word. Isn't it beautiful that Jesus is the sent Word that was sent from heaven? The Jewish people of that day still held to the paper and ink prophecies and when the Sent One showed up they wouldn't accept Him. They kept going back to the paper and the ink. They hung on to the scrolls and ignored the one the scrolls were talking about. God doesn't want us to become religious. He wants us to become real.

When you read the book you have to understand that God is talking to you in a *logos* way, but He wants to make it real, a sent word, a *rhema* to you. The *logos* will lead you to a *rhema*. It will lead you to a sent word, a sent One. Then the Word becomes flesh in your life.

Jesus was the sent Word and He always spoke the sent Word. What came out of Him was not flesh, not memorized scriptures. I know of people who have the scriptures memorized. Scripture memorization is a good thing if you ever take it to heart. But to just, by rote memory, parrot something out doesn't mean there is any power in that whatsoever. I have seen people on the streets, total alcoholics who could quote more scripture than people in church but there was no power, no life in it. If there was life in it they wouldn't be on the streets bound by alcohol because the power of the sent Word would have set them free a long time ago.

To know about something doesn't mean that you have the revelation of it. That's why it is important for us to understand it is okay to hear something you have heard before. It is very wrong for us to sit back and say we have heard it all before. There is a fresh revelation with every scripture, so many revelations that you could spend eternity with one verse. God will constantly be giving you new meat on it.

I have preached some scriptures that I have preached on before but there is a new revelation, a new slant, new meat. There is a new flow on many of the scriptures that I look at now. I see them totally different. They are fuller, more complete.

Several years ago I thought I knew everything in the Bible on confession of the Word, the power of your tongue and all of that. We can get so religiously cocky that we shut somebody down who is trying to share the Word with us. We feel like we know it all. That kind of attitude stops revelation. Well, my mother pulled out a verse on me about confession and blew me away. It was an angle that I had never seen before. The Lord gave me a little spanking on that and told me that I didn't know it all. I thought I had that one little verse all down pat. God will do that to all of us. There is no room for religious pride.

Paul speaks about the unsearchable riches found in Christ. That means that for all of eternity Jesus is going to be revealing another part of Himself, another revelation about Himself. It is going to happen forever. We will never be bored. Revelation is exciting. Every time the Lord shows me something new, I get excited. It is fresh, wonderful. There is power in it. It is the sent word. There is life in it. And to think that for all eternity, Jesus is constantly going to reveal Himself to us. Whatever He reveals to us we enter into it even more. We think that when we get there we have it all. No, we have Him who is all.

We are not just going to sit there and pluck on a harp. There is work to be done. We are going to rule and reign over the universe with

Him as kings and priests unto Him. If you are going to be a king and priest that means you are going to be placed in a position over somebody in some place. We are going to have assignments throughout eternity. There is going to be a lot of work to do. We are going to rule and reign in the universe with the Lord.

Think about it – from the time He said, *"Let there be..."* the universe has been expanding at 186,000 miles per second. That is how quick it has been going forward, how quick it has been created and it never stops. God stepped back for one day to look at what He had done. Then He jumped back in there to keep creating. There are galaxies, worlds. Scientists do not know the end of the universe. It has been expanding quickly from the time God said, *"Let there be..."* and we do not know how many billions of years this has been going on. We know that mankind has been around for about 6,000 years. But we don't know about all of creation or the part before creation. We may think it was a day but it might have been a billion years. We can speculate, but a day is as a thousand years and a thousand years as a day. So, how can we really know?

John 6:63; *"It is the spirit that quickeneth* [makes alive or activates]*; the flesh profiteth nothing: <u>the words that I speak unto you</u> [sent words], they are spirit, and they are life."*

To paraphrase John, *"I am speaking by the Spirit of God. I am giving you a sent word and it is spirit and life. The words that I speak are spirit and life."*

Think about it – the spirit quickens. What if you and I were spending time with God, seeking the Lord, feeding and seeding and asking God for a sent word? He gives us a sent word and we speak only the sent word. It is the spirit that quickens, the flesh profits nothing. The words that you begin to speak are words of spirit and life. The spirit will flow, produce the seed and activate the power within the word. God is trying to teach us that we need to quit being religious and be very much dependent on Him for everything. We need to realize we have to have Him. We are comatose without the Holy Ghost. We can't do anything without Him. We need the Spirit of God. It is the Spirit that quickeneth, which means to activate or bring to life. A seed has to be quickened.

Potential to Produce

Remember the parable of the sower of the seed being in the ground? The seeds that go into the ground have to be quickened or brought to life, activated. Just seed in dirt has no life. You can put the best seed in the richest soil, but without water you have nothing. You have the potential for something because the seed has all the potential to produce. This written Word (the Bible) has all the potential to produce.

For years we preached potential as if it were kinetic energy, but the laws of inertia tell us that there is potential energy and kinetic energy. Potential energy is energy that is harnessed and stored but not released. It does nothing though it has potential. Kinetic energy is energy where the power in it is released outward to do something. The written word is potential energy. But it takes the Spirit of God to activate it and turn it from potential energy to kinetic energy, energy that is released to do something. There is potential energy, potential miracles in the written word for everything you and I will ever need. But many people who have Bibles do not have miracles. There are probably more who don't have miracles than those who do, though all have the potential for them.

It is a big mistake to think potential energy and kinetic energy are the same thing. That is called presumption. Presumption will make you think you have something when you don't. You will try to act on it, walk on it and nothing will ever take place. Becoming disillusioned with God and His Word, you begin to believe the doubts of the enemy about the Word of God and about God's ability.

The kinetic word is all the power you will ever need. Remember, the potential word has the power locked up in it, but it is not released. There are people trying to make the potential word work for them and it isn't. Satan uses that to instill fear, doubt and unbelief in their lives. Whereas the kinetic word is the release of everything it says.

Isaiah 55:11; *"So shall my word be that goeth forth out of my mouth: it shall not return unto me void, but it shall accomplish that which I please, and it shall prosper in the thing whereto I sent it."*

It shall not return void because of the Spirit of God. That is why I am comatose without the Holy Ghost. I need the Holy Ghost to unlock the potential power located in the Word and make it kinetic so that whatever I need is flowing freely and being released to me now in tangibility. The Bible speaks about the incorruptible seed.

2 Peter 1:16-19; *"For we have not followed cunningly devised fables, when we made known unto you the power and coming of our Lord Jesus Christ, but were eyewitnesses of his majesty. For he received from God the Father honour and glory, when there came such a voice to him from the excellent glory,* [Here comes a sent word.] ***This is my beloved Son, in whom I am well pleased. And this voice which came from heaven we heard, when we were with him in the holy mount. We have also a more sure word of prophecy; whereunto ye do well that ye take heed, as unto a light that shineth in a dark place, until the day dawn, and the day star arise in your hearts:"***

This is speaking about the potential word becoming kinetic. You have to stay with the Word of God. You have to stay with the potential Word, which means read it, study it and meditate on it. Add to it prayer.

Prayer is yielding to the water, yielding to the Holy Ghost. Any time scripture is speaking about water it is speaking about the Spirit of God. It takes water to germinate the seed. Water unlocks the potential power so that it becomes kinetic or activated.

Every time you meditate on the Word, every time you pray over the scriptures and seek the Lord in His Word with prayer you are giving heed. Keep giving heed until the day dawn. The day dawn is the dawning of the day that the miracle is released. *"And the day star rise in your heart."* The daystar is Jesus. This means until the revelation of Jesus rises up in your spirit, which is what brings the day dawn, the dawning of the day that your miracle takes place.

2 Peter 1:20; *"Knowing this first, that no prophecy of the scripture is of any private interpretation."*

Peter is saying that anybody who wants the Spirit of God to unveil the Word can get it. It is not just a private interpretation just for one person. *"Well, that one person got a now word from God and they got a miracle. I guess he is the only one who will."* No, there is no private interpretation here or private unlocking of the potential power for just one. It is for everyone.

2 Peter 1:21; *"For the prophecy came not in old time by the will of man: but holy men of God spake as they were moved by the Holy Ghost."*

They were moved by the Holy Ghost and brought forth an appointed word. How do you bring forth an appointed word? By the Spirit of God.

There is an appointed word. It is not void of power. It brings forth miracles. The appointed word changes our lives. The appointed word brings prosperity into every area of our life. The appointed word brings forth an accomplishment of what it says.

Be thankful for the bibles that you have. But don't be religious to the point of thinking that the paper, the ink and the leather have power in themselves. It is the meaning of the words. Sleeping with your bible will not make you more holy. Putting it under your pillow will not cause your mind to be healed. Throwing a bible on a demon-possessed person will not set them free unless the Spirit of God tells you to do that. A demon-possessed person will rip a bible to shreds unless the Spirit of God tells you to put it on them.

We respect the bible very highly, but what we respect more than anything is the sent word, the word activated, the walking bible. We respect the *logos* knowing that the *logos* will be transformed into the *rhema* by the Spirit of God. The meaning in my heart will produce the blessing in my life. It will manifest.

The Word is about to become flesh to you and manifest. How do you get it? You keep giving heed to the scripture and praying. Keep feeding, praying, waiting on the Spirit of God because He will bring it forth. He will activate and bring forth an interpretation, a sent word, a revelation. When that comes forth whatever is revealed is what will manifest. It is the Word that will become flesh.

Fully Complete

I believe you can come to the place where you are thoroughly furnished in every area of your life because you know how to receive a sent word. You know how to position yourself for a sent word. You know how to get a sent word.

2 Timothy 3:16-17; *"All scripture is given by inspiration of God, and is profitable for doctrine, for reproof, for correction, for instruction in righteousness: That the man of God may be perfect* [complete]*, thoroughly furnished unto all good works."*

"Complete" means whatever you need is already supplied in full. *"Shalom,"* peace, means complete, thoroughly furnished in every area of your life, equipped. There is not a lack in any area in any realm. There is not a lack of finances. There is not a lack of anointing. There is not a lack of wisdom. There is not a lack of blessing in the home. No lack of blessing in any area in any realm to any degree. That is God's desire for us.

All scripture that is released as a sent word will do that. All fresh scripture does that. All fresh manna does that. All fresh word does that. It is all *rhema* words that do that.

Our greatest need is to have the seed brought to life just as if God spoke it for the very first time to you, as if you were the only reason He ever said it. That is a *rhema*. This is good meat and it will feed you if you will let it. That is why I can tell you I don't have the total handle on this. I have some of it and I am getting more of it. I can't say that I am totally complete yet or thoroughly furnished. I am heading that way. The more this is unveiled to me, the more I can enter into it because the power to perceive and receive whatever is released is there. The more that this is real to us the more we can enter into it. The more we enter, the more complete we become without lacking anything. I want to be complete, thoroughly furnished to do every good thing I should be doing. I won't lack anointing. I won't lack money. I won't lack strength. I won't lack health. I will have everything I need to do everything I am supposed to do in the earth. That means there is no hindrance.

It is the scripture revealed. It is the *rhema* of the word. It is the sent word. It is the Holy Ghost germinating and bringing to life the potential of the written word so that it becomes kinetic, released energy and released power to become everything it says so that we are complete not lacking anything, so we have everything we need to do everything we are supposed to do.

Isaiah 55:6-8; *"Seek ye the LORD while he may be found, call ye upon him while he is near: Let the wicked forsake his way, and the unrighteous man his thoughts: and let him return unto the LORD, and he will have mercy upon him; and to our God, for he will abundantly pardon. For my thoughts are not your thoughts, neither are your ways my ways, saith the LORD."*

But God wants that to change. He was telling it the way it was at that moment. The reason everything was put in written form was so that our thoughts could become His thoughts and our ways become His ways. First thoughts then ways, did you notice that? You have to change your thinking before you can change your action. That is why it is so important to get the revealed word taught and preached to us. It will change our thinking, thereby changing our actions thereby changing the results. We need the Word of God.

Isaiah 55:9-10; *"For as the heavens are higher than the earth, so are my ways higher than your ways, and my thoughts than your thoughts. For as the rain cometh down, and the snow from heaven, and returneth not thither, but watereth the earth, and maketh it bring forth and bud, that it may give seed to the sower, and bread to the eater:"*

Remember what we said about the water (rain). To understand this better, look at the parable of the sower in Matthew 13. Jesus said that the ground, the earth, was the heart. Isaiah said that the rain waters the earth and makes it bring forth and bud that it may give seed to the sower and bread to the eater. This is describing exactly what I have been saying about the sent word.

You need to feed and seed this into your heart. But you have to have the Holy Ghost – the water of the Spirit – to germinate it, to bring it forth and bud. The word will not produce until it has first been germinated by the rain and the water of the Spirit of God.

It is like the preaching of the word. If I just grabbed any old message and read some scriptures to you I would not be giving you a *rhema*. I am only giving you a *logos* word. If you haven't prayed or done anything else, then the good seed will fall on a heart that has no water. The seed will be there but nothing is ever produced. You will never see anything happening in your life for God.

That is why it doesn't benefit some people to go to some churches. They will hear a dry word that is going to fall on a dry heart, which means no germination and no fruit. Prayer and connecting with the Holy Ghost, meditating, feeding and seeding on the Word will make all the difference in a minister. When I am giving you something I am giving you a seed that has already been soaked in water. It already has a start. If you will yield to the Holy Ghost, He will water you a lot more. You will have a quick return, a quick manifestation.

Isaiah 55:10-11; *"For as the rain cometh down, and the snow from heaven, and returneth not thither, but watereth the earth, and maketh it bring forth and bud, that it may give seed to the sower, and bread to the eater: So shall my word be that goeth forth out of my mouth: it shall not return unto me void, but it shall accomplish that which I please, and it shall prosper in the thing whereto I sent it."*

The water makes seed bring forth and bud. The seed can't make it happen. Water germinated the seed. Water was the key that unlocked the potential power in the seed and caused it to bud, to bring forth the power. A seed of healing needs water as the key to unlock it so that a person can get healed. A seed of prosperity needs water to unlock it so that a person will prosper.

"For as the rain cometh down" is the movement of the Spirit through prayer and seeking God. Hosea 10:12 says that we are to break up the fallow ground and seek the Lord until He comes and rains

righteousness upon us. Through repentance and prayer we position ourselves for a downpour. We position ourselves for the rain to come.

How do you get a sent word? You have to get ready for the rain. You need the key, which is the rain of the Spirit. The downpour of the Spirit unlocks the seed that produces the harvest of whatever the seed says that it is. There is healing seed in the Word of God. There is deliverance seed, prosperity seed, intimacy seed, salvation seed, wholeness seed, peace seed, and holiness seed in the Word of God. I could go on and on and on. It is all there. There is the fullness of the Spirit seed. The power is locked up in the written word. Through the key of the Spirit and the water of the Spirit that power is unlocked and released so that we may enjoy its full potential. It makes us want to have a marriage of prayer and the Word together. It is not all Spirit and not all Word. It is Spirit and Word.

Everything in life is produced through the germination factor and the seed coming together. Nothing in this earth in the natural or in the Spirit is ever produced without the coming together of those two. So, why do we think that just the seed of the Word is going to do it? That seed has to be germinated by the Spirit of God in us. The Word has to become flesh in order for that promise to dwell among us. Are you ready for the manifestation of all of your family members saved walking among you? Are you ready for the manifestation of all the power of God walking among you? Are you ready for the manifestation of full prosperity walking among you? How about full health? Full deliverance? Full wholeness and healing? You can become complete and fully furnished to accomplish everything you need to do without lack in anything.

The Sent Word Produces Faith

Psalms 78:41; *"Yea, they turned back and tempted God, and limited the Holy One of Israel."*

The word *"limited"* here means to put a cap on, to cap off what you receive from God. You limit what God can do. As individuals we can stop God from being God. The limitation is that of stopping our own receiving from Him.

About 3.5 million people came out of Israel. The Bible tells us in Psalm 105:37 that He brought them forth with silver and with gold, not in poverty. There wasn't one feeble among their tribes. In other words, they were rich and healthy. Look at the number of hospitals we have in our cities and then imagine what it was like to have 3.5 million people healthy and able to walk out of Egypt.

They carried out wealth. According to Exodus 12, they spoiled the Egyptians by demanding all the goods that had been taken from them for 400 years. That was quite a stash. They carried out the silver and the gold, necklaces, bracelets, earrings, and anklets. The men carried about 120 pounds of gold each. The woman carried around 80 pounds. They were wearing this gold out of Egypt. That is how much wealth there was.

They walked out of Egypt carrying their wealth and healthy in their body. God brought forth His people with joy, His chosen with gladness.[6] They came out rejoicing, happy in their God. It is important for us to understand that later they began to limit what they could receive from God. Down the road when trials began to come, when lack began to attack, they couldn't find water. They were thirsty. At Marah they found water, but it was bitter. So they began to complain instead of praising, rejoicing in the fact that the God who could bring them out of Egypt surely could provide a little drink of water.

---

[6] Psalm 105

Think of all the miracles that had already happened. The Passover alone caused the Pharaoh, who was hard at heart, to tell them to get out of his sight. They had all walked out healed and very wealthy. When they come to the Red Sea, the power of God parted it for them. Miracle after miracle after miracle.

There is a problem many times with our receiving a miracle before we have developed faith. There is a difference between the gifts of the Spirit operating and by faith taking hold of a miracle. I have been in services where there have been times the Spirit of God was doing something and it had nothing to do with the faith of the people. It was just the Spirit of God doing something. That is okay except that if we live by the gifts of the Spirit we will begin to act no different than the children of Israel.

The just shall live by faith.[7] We have to develop our faith in Almighty God and thank Him for those times He sovereignly moves by the gifts of the Spirit. But there will also be times when you can't seem to get God to move through the gifts of the Spirit. Does that mean that during those seasons we are going to have lack, have dryness, go through something and God does not move on your behalf?

No, not at all. Faith in God can move a mighty mountain. Through faith you can always and at all times get an answer, get a miracle, have God move on your behalf. You can walk by faith. You can live by faith. You can trust God for your daily bread. You can trust God to meet you everyday. You can trust Him to be your healer and your deliverer moment by moment, day by day. Faith will always work when the gifts of the Spirit won't.

That is why I don't just go into churches and flow in the gifts. I would be crippling you. I would be setting you up for the same fall the children of Israel went through. There are churches that want me to come in and do my *thing*. They don't want me to preach. They want me to come in and prophesy, move in the gifts, get some teeth filled, get some miracles happening, get some prophetic words going, thrill somebody and get somebody pumped.

---

[7] Romans 1:17

But I won't be with them the next day when they face some devil. Next week I am going on down the road. What are they going to do when I am not there? But, I can build your faith in the Word of God. I can take you to God. I can take you to His Word. I can get you plugged in so that when I am gone you are still plugged into His Word and you can receive from Him. God's Word is first and foremost to me. His Word is everything to me. If I don't preach the Word, then I don't know why I am there.

I have seen people get healed by the preaching of the Word. I have seen them delivered by the preaching of the Word. I have seen them set free by the preaching of the Word. I have seen them get hold of the truth and down the road they got a miracle when I wasn't there.

Once I have preached the Word, instilled that in you and the Holy Spirit wants to move in the gifts, I will flow in that. I want to. I enjoy that. I remember times when I pastored that the prophetic was very strong. We flowed in the gifts. But there were services where the Holy Spirit only wanted me to preach. I didn't dare prophesy that day. The Spirit of God told me that if I prophesied to them every Sunday, every service, I would cripple them. They would never learn to hear God for themselves. All they would want would be for me to prophesy.

The children of Israel fell so easy because they did not have the Word in them. Everything was based on the miracles that God performed through Moses. They didn't use any faith. They let Moses do it all. They let God do it all and that is why they fell in the wilderness. The majority of them, except for Joshua and Caleb, died in the wilderness and never went into the promises of God.

We have to develop our faith in the Word of God. Thank God for the gifts. Thank God for the prophetic. The Lord will confirm His Word with signs following. But that is the thing, He will *confirm* His Word. The Word has to be there. I like to preach the Word and yield to the Spirit of God. I like to see the Lord put His stamp of approval on what has been preached, but I want the Word of God to be first and foremost in my life and in the lives of those I am ministering to. I never want them to look at me and put me on a pedestal of worship because I don't deserve that.

Respect – that's great. Worship – no. Worship God. I have to go to God just like you do.

Sometimes people think that ministers go to heaven during the week and float down at service time. I am just like you. I can get hurt. I get hungry at times, tired at times. Believe it or not, I get discouraged at times. I have to go to the Word and get encouraged. It is asked, who ministers to the minister. The preachers have to know where to go. We go to God and we reach out to each other many times for ministry and encouragement.

Thank God for prophetic words, but thank God for the more sure Word of prophecy that you do well to take heed unto until the day dawn and the day star arises in your heart.[8] It is important we see that this is the more sure word of prophecy. It is the one you can always, always count on. I might miss it. Someone else might miss it. But God's Word will never miss it. There have been times when I have prophesied to somebody and thought it was for them when it was actually for one of their family members. When I prophesy I try not to be like a bull in a china closet coming on strong and knocking everyone down with how great I am. That attitude is not the attitude of the Spirit of the Lord. That is all flesh. There is nothing wrong with boldness as long as within the boldness there is still gentleness. Where is the fruit of the Spirit?[9]

Israel limited the Holy One of Israel. They capped off or stopped the flow in their behalf. I believe it was because of their unbelief. They were looking at signs and wonders and not trusting in the nature and character of God. I can say that because the Word of God says the people knew the works of God, but Moses knew His ways. Moses knew His ways means he knew the character of God. He knew why God does what He does. It was because of His personality. Israel only knew the works of God and so when they didn't receive the works of God then all of a sudden they had no faith in God.

---

[8] 2 Peter 1:19

[9] We talk about the nine gifts but what about the nine fruit? There is a fruit that connects with every gift that causes God to get the glory. If you have the gift without the fruit you get the glory and God doesn't. This teaching is covered in the second year of the School of the Prophets.

The power of God is in knowing what to put your faith in. You don't put your faith in the power of God. You put your faith in the nature of God. The nature will determine whether or not you get a blessing, whether or not you get healed, whether or not you get saved, whether or not you get delivered. You trust the nature of God. Demons believe and tremble. They know God has power, but that doesn't get them saved. That doesn't get them to heaven. It is not believing in His power. I will tell you why. Stop and think about it for a moment.

If one of my children came up to me and said that they believed I could buy them a pair of shoes, but they didn't know if I would, that would hurt deeply. They have not learned to trust my nature and character.

There are people who will say they know God can do great things. They believe He can, but they don't believe He will. They are just like the children of Israel. They are looking at the acts, looking the works, but they don't know the nature.

Acts 10:38; *"How God anointed Jesus of Nazareth with the Holy Ghost and with power: who went about doing good, and healing all that were oppressed of the devil; for God was with him."*

Why did Jesus do good? When you stop and check out the Word of God you will find out that God is a good God. We have to get to know the goodness of God. It is the goodness of God that leads men to repentance.[10] Put faith and trust in the willingness of God, the nature of God is what brings the promised blessings and not in the ability of God.

Proverbs 3:5; *"Trust in the LORD with all thine heart; and lean not unto thine own understanding."*

"Lord" means the one who is over you, the one you have submitted to, the one who is in lordship over you. Your lord is the one you are in relationship with. In medieval times, the lord over a particular land was the one who would take care of everybody else, oversee everything and make sure everything was handled.

---

[10] Romans 2:4

Proverbs 3:6; *"In all thy ways acknowledge him, and he shall direct thy paths."*

What are you acknowledging? That He is a good God, that He is the lover of your soul. He cares for you. He provides for you. He wants you blessed. His plans are to prosper you, give you a future and an expected end. It is not to do you evil or harm, but to do you good. You have to get to know that and put faith in it. It is faith in the goodness of God, in the character of God. My children know that if they need anything they can come to me. Their daddy is a good daddy. I do buy them shoes. I do buy them clothes. I do provide for them and I usually give them extra along the way. They know I am good to them. They can put their trust in the goodness. They don't always know when I have got it and when I don't. But they can still trust the goodness.

God always has it. That means you can always get it.

Are you trusting His power or His goodness? Stop and think about it.

People who are trusting the power of God will not always have a miracle. People who are trusting the nature of God will. Once you get that in your spirit, it will do something for you. The children of Israel didn't trust God. They knew He was a God of power and might. They had seen it. They saw all the miracles in Egypt. They saw awesome power through Moses. They saw Moses take his staff, throw it down and it became a snake. The magicians did the same thing but the rod of Moses ate the others up. They watched him stick his hand in his bosom, pull it out and it was leprous. Put his hand back in, pull it out and it was just like a baby's skin. They watched all of that. They watched each and every one of the plagues that were brought on by the man of God speaking what God said. They watched the greatest god of Egypt die. Pharaoh's son was reverenced as god incarnate in the flesh. That is why when the son of Pharaoh died, Pharaoh gave up. When their ultimate god died, there was nothing to do but give up.

The Israelites watched God perform all of these things. They watched God heal everybody and prosper everybody in one day. They all walked out healthy. They watched the Red Sea part. They watched each one of these miracles: the manna that came down on the ground, the clothes that never wore out, water coming out of a rock. They saw miracle after miracle after miracle.

But seeing a miracle is not enough to give us faith to see continued miracles. I have been in services where there were miracles, but the next week some of the people could not trust God to meet the smallest need. It wasn't their faith that got those things flowing in the first place. They were just witnessing it. Miracles are a sign to lead people to the Lord. The Bible never says that a sign and a wonder produce faith. Signs and wonders are a dinner bell to wake people up to see that maybe there is a God. Miracles are wake up calls. The miracles themselves do not produce faith. What produces faith is the Word of God.

Faith in God's Word

Romans 10:17; *"So then faith cometh by hearing, and hearing by the word of God."*

"Word" is defined as a *rhema*, a revelation, hearing an illumination, having the Word of God come alive to you while it is being preached. That is what produces faith. When you hear a fresh word, faith comes. When the word of God is preached, fresh faith comes. A sent word produces faith. The appointed word produces faith. We are thankful for miracles, but miracles don't produce faith.

If you really want to do this thing right, you need to put faith in God's Word. Then God's Word will produce miracles. You would have a miracle every day, if you needed it, with the Word of God, with the *rhema* of the Word, with a sent word. A sent word is a revelation word, an appointed word, a word that God speaks to you fresh up out of His Word. When you get a sent word, hearing that sent word produces faith.

Abraham didn't have written scripture. He had something even better – God's voice direct.

God takes the Word and speaks it as if it were the first time He ever spoke it to anybody. You get that through reading and meditating on the Word. You need to feed and seed it into your spirit. You pray over it and ask God to give you a sent word, a revelation. When He begins to give you a revelation the bubble up comes because you have been feeding and seeding, meditating. You feed the word in your spirit, the Spirit of God takes hold of what you have been feeding on and He uses whatever is there to give you what you really need. It will bubble up and when it does, it is a sent word. It might come in the middle of the night. You are facing trouble, wake up and here comes a scripture alive to you. Faith comes by hearing and hearing by the Word of God. You just heard God.

Some people don't know that they are hearing God when they are because God speaks through His Word. Many times while you are reading it something leaps off the page. You just heard God. You just got a sent word. Driving down the road, a verse of scripture bubbles up – you have just heard God. That is a sent word and faith is there. Anytime the scriptures start coming to you, bubbling up, faith is there. God is talking. Are you listening?

That in itself is all you need to produce any miracle that your heart desires. It is not hard to hear God. You just have to know how He speaks. You have to know that He doesn't speak the same way we do. He doesn't boom loud stuff the same way we do all the time. Sometimes it is that still small voice. Sometimes it is a gentle prompting. Sometimes it is the knowings, the stirrings. It is the scripture that keeps popping up inside of you, keeps coming into your mind. It is that impression that keeps coming up.

Sometimes we wonder what is wrong with us, we keep getting the same thought. What is wrong is that we are not getting what God is saying to us. We think, *"It is just me. What is wrong with me?"* God is trying to tell you something. You keep having an impression about somebody in your life, somebody you have been praying for. Later on you find out something happened to them. They were in an accident or something went wrong. Then you understand, but you had put it off to just being you. We think the only way God can speak to us is the way the preacher talks to us, using audible words that we can hear. I want to tell you that He very seldom ever talks to me that way. I have heard the audible voice of God, but that is not the regular thing. Most of the time it is the inner witness, the gentle prompting, a scripture that floats up very gently, an impression that is so gentle I could just let it slide. I could just say it is me.

Deuteronomy 8:1-2; *"All the commandments which I command thee this day shall ye observe to do, that ye may live, and multiply, and go in and possess the land which the LORD sware unto your fathers. And thou shalt remember all the way which the LORD thy God led thee these forty years in the wilderness, to humble thee, and to prove thee, <u>to know what was in thine heart</u>, whether thou wouldest keep his commandments, or no."*

The Bible tells us that the heart of man is deceitful. We think many times that we have everything all smoothed over and everything is just right. How many times does a little pressure come our way and something come up out of us that we didn't think was there? We thought we had that under the blood.

Deuteronomy 8:3; *"And he humbled thee, and suffered thee to hunger, and fed thee with manna, which thou knewest not, neither did thy fathers know; that he might make thee know that man doth not live by bread only, but by every word that proceedeth out of the mouth of the LORD doth man live."*

"Word" (Hebrew: *dabar, daw-bar'*) is the revealed word, the sent word. We live by the revealed word, the sent word.

The Title Deed

God gave the Israelites manna every day instead of putting grocery stores along their path. He did it on purpose so that they would trust His word. So that they would know that if He said it, He would do it. God was saying that the fact He said it is what produced it. You have to trust that. The fact that He sent the word is proof enough that it will manifest. If He hadn't said it then you know it wouldn't happen. Because He said it, that is the only evidence you need.

Hebrews 11:1; *"Now faith is the substance of things hoped for, the evidence of things not seen."*

One translation says that faith is the title deed. It is like someone sending you a deed to a piece of property that you have never seen. It is still yours. The way you know it is because you have the deed. You have the word on it.

Faith is in the fact that God said it. When God says something it is the title deed. When He sends you a word that is title deed. When He said to Abraham, *"You are the father of many nations"* it was a title deed. God had already signed the contract when He said it.

My grandpa talked about this. He told me that many years ago you could walk into the bank and did not need a contract like we do today. All you had to do was go in, tell them how much money you needed and tell them that you would pay it. They would give you the money. He never signed one contract because his word was enough.

God's Word is enough. His Word is the signed contract. What He says produces what He says because His Words are a creative force. When He spoke the universe into existence, He didn't have to prove to the elements that He was God. He just spoke and the elements were formed. He hasn't quit being the creator. He is still the creator. He only rested for one day. So whatever He tells you, His saying it creates it. All you have to do to see that creative force released is believe in it and add patience to your faith.

Deuteronomy 8:3; *"…that he might make thee know that man doth not live by bread only, but by every word that proceedeth out of the mouth of the LORD doth man live."*

In other words, God was saying that your livelihood, your ability to eat is based on God saying He would feed you. Your ability to have money is because He said He would supply all your needs. That is a creative word. We don't understand that because today nobody's word is good. And because nobody's word is good we don't understand how God's Word can be so good. If we were in a society where every man's word was their bond, where a person was good only if their word was good, where when someone said something and their character was good, everybody believed them, their word carried power, we would understand

God's Word. But because nobody's word means a thing anymore we don't understand how God's Word can mean something.

God creates with what He says. Hebrews tells us that if He says it He is the surety of the New Covenant. He backs His word. He stands behind every word. If He says it, He makes it good. This should make you want to study, meditate and read the Word more until something jumps off the page at you. The moment it jumps off the page at you, comes to you in the middle of the night, becomes real to you – at that moment it is creative and you are going to get it.

This is a deep word, but it is not a word that you can't reach.

God says that He led them into the wilderness and fed them with manna on purpose just so they would know that His speaking about provision would produce provision.

Have you ever had God speak a word from the scriptures to you? Ever had a verse of scripture keep coming to you? You know the power in it right then by the fact it came to you by the Holy Ghost. It became a *rhema*. Creative power is there. What kind of creative power? Power to create what was the context of that scripture.

Isaiah 55:10-11; *"For as the rain cometh down, and the snow from heaven, and returneth not thither, but watereth the earth, and maketh it bring forth and bud, that it may give seed to the sower, and bread to the eater: So shall my word be that goeth forth out of my mouth: it <u>shall not return unto me void</u>, but it <u>shall accomplish that which I please</u>, and it <u>shall prosper in the thing whereto I sent it</u>."*

Notice the three things the sent word is going to do. First, it will not return void, which means there will be fruit. Fruit means that whatever it says will happen. It will bear fruit. No word of God is void of power. No *rhema* of God is void of power. No *dabar* of God is void of power. No sent word of God is void of power. The creative power is in it. You and I need to put our trust in God's nature and in His character knowing He cannot fail. He cannot lie. He loves us and cares for us. Trust His Word. Know that there is creative power in His Word. You have to know that. It will not return void.

Second, God's Word will accomplish something that pleases Him when it is accomplished. He sends the Word to make something come alive, to accomplish something in your life. *"I need healing. I need finances. I need to see my family saved."* Your greatest need is for the revelation of the Word.

Third, the revelation of the Word will produce all those things, and a whole lot more. What good is it to get a little more money, but not have a revelation? You are going to turn around and have the same need again. You have to have a revelation, which means a fresh word from God out of His scripture. God's greatest pleasure and desire is for the Word to be spoken fresh to you because then the power of it is released into your daily life.

Prayer in the Holy Spirit

Do you know why we need to pray a lot in the Holy Ghost?

Praying in tongues is not something you put up on the mantle and say, *"Here is the time I spoke in tongues. I am a tongue talker (or at least I was)."* Some folks put it up on the mantle as a trophy of something they attained in God. No, it is a tool of blessing for us.

Praying in the Holy Ghost is building yourself up on your most holy faith.[11] Smith Wigglesworth had a saying, *"Some people read the Bible in the Hebrew, and some read it in the Greek. I learned to read the Bible in the Holy Ghost."* I showed you earlier that when you pray in tongues your spirit prays but your understanding is unfruitful. In other words, it doesn't take your mind to pray in tongues. It is not of your natural mind, it is of your spirit. The Amplified Bible in 1 Corinthians 14:14-15 says that my spirit prays by the Holy Spirit that is within me, within my spirit. The Holy Spirit in my spirit gives me the unction, gives me the words to speak and then my spirit man prays them out. My natural man picks up on it and releases it.

---

[11] We have a manual called <u>Supernatural Prayer Produces Supernatural Results</u> which talks about the power of praying in tongues, how to enter into what is available to you.

Do you understand who wrote the Bible? *"Holy men of old spake as they were moved by the Holy Ghost."*[12] *"All scripture is given by inspiration of God."*[13] It came from the Spirit of God. When you pray in tongues you pray by the Spirit of God who is within you.

I learned how to take passages of scripture that I didn't have light on, start praying in the Holy Ghost and then read them slowly while I was praying in tongues softly. While I am doing that, all of a sudden they are leaping off the page at me. Unbelievable *rhema*. While it is leaping off the page the creative power of it is being released into my life. No word is void of power. All of His Word is creative. There is not a word in the Bible that is not creative. Then why don't more people get the blessing out of it? Because all they are reading is the *logos*, they are not getting the *rhema* out of it. It is through the *rhema* that the power of it is released into your life. So, what will happen if you add the missing ingredient, the Spirit of God? The water will germinate the seed. The *logos* is the dry seed, the Holy Ghost is the water.

Do you want what is in the Bible to come forth to you as life?

Isaiah 55:10-11; *"For as the rain* [every time the Bible speaks about rain it is speaking about the Holy Ghost] ***cometh down, and the snow from heaven, and returneth not thither, but watereth the earth*** [our hearts]***, and <u>maketh it bring forth and bud</u>, that it may give seed to the sower, and bread to the eater*** [That means there will be a release of power. It will produce and I will get to eat it.]***: So shall my word be that goeth forth out of my mouth: it shall not return unto me void, but it shall accomplish that which I please, and it shall prosper in the thing whereto I sent it."***

In Matthew 13 the soil, spoken of in the parable of the sower, is our heart. The seed is the Word of God. When we tie the parable of the sower in with Isaiah 55, we can say the rain of the Spirit that comes down is what causes the seed to bring forth. The Word will produce, by the Holy Ghost, rain and I will get to eat the results of what happens when it buds and brings forth. That means I will get to eat prosperity. It will start happening in my life. I will get to eat healing which means healing will

---

[12] 2 Peter 1:21
[13] 2 Timothy 3:16

start happening in my life. I get to eat being anointed and being blessed because when that seed comes forth by the Holy Ghost it will bring forth and bud so that somebody can eat it.

That is why I believe we don't need to read the Word without prayer. Nor do we need to pray without the Word. The two should be coupled together. You will have to really get into the Spirit to be able to do this. I found out the first few times I tried it was hard on my flesh. I had to concentrate, press into God, release tongues, let them flow and then just follow along in the Word. I had to let my mind be anointed as my eyes followed along in the Word, praying in the Holy Ghost until stuff started coming alive and being germinated by the water of the Spirit. I dare you to try it with even one small passage of three or four verses. I dare you to pray in the Holy Ghost and read them over and over. Read them over several times. I dare you to do this every day for a week and see if the revelation of the Word hasn't increased many times over. See if you don't get an understanding of the Word that you didn't have before.

Send Now Prosperity

God's Word concerning prosperity is about much more than money. It is about fulfilling destiny. If you have been destined to be a soul winner, you need to prosper in that. If you have been destined to have a business, you need to prosper in that. If you have been destined to be a good mother or a good father, you need to prosper in that. If you have been destined to be married, you need to prosper in that. If you have been destined to be single, you need to prosper in that. Whatever you have been destined to do, prosperity brings you to success in God.

"I don't understand this prosperity stuff." Wait a minute, you need to go back and see what God's prosperity is. It is different from what we think. If your definition of prosperity is for greed, just for money so you can get things, then I don't believe in that kind of prosperity. That is not Bible prosperity.

There are two extremes I have seen over the years. One is that poverty means you are spiritual. That is wrong. Years ago there were people who would take vows of poverty. It was supposed to make them very spiritual. But it doesn't. It is a lie. It is not in the Word of God. Then there are people who have equated gain with godliness. And that is not right either. 1 Timothy 6:5 talks about those who think gain is godliness. Just because I have things does not make me more spiritual than somebody else. Driving a nice car doesn't mean I have more faith than somebody else. The kinds of clothes I wear do not make me more spiritual than somebody else. Paul said to run from those who think gain is godliness, flee from them.[14] Yet, we see there are some people who believe that.

So, we understand there is a balance to everything. As long as we stay with God's Word, we are all right. That is why we should be students of the Word. Don't just take everything you hear preached. You must

---

[14] 1Timothy 6:5

study the Word of God for yourself. Remember to get your definitions from the Word of God.

Psalms 118:25; *"Save now, I beseech thee, O LORD: O LORD, I beseech thee, send now prosperity."*

"Send" really means to appoint. The only way that God can send you prosperity is to send you a word about prosperity. God can't get anything to you without His Word. His Word is the device that He uses to get to you, to give to you anything and everything He wants to bless you with. He cannot bless you without first saying it. He didn't even create the world without first saying it. To speak a word, He had to send a word. God can't do anything in your behalf without sending a word.

It was prophesied thousands of years before it happened that God was sending a Messiah, prophesied over and over by the prophets. God had to say it. His saying it produces it. We don't always understand that. If we can ever get a grip on that we will live a life of faith and walk in total victory. The centurion understood that. He told Jesus to just speak the Word. Jesus didn't have to come and do a thing. All He had to do was speak the Word and it would get done. Jesus said that was the greatest faith He had ever seen in all of Israel. He got so excited. How would you like to have the kind of faith that would make God say, *"Wow?"* You can. Catch the concept that the Word is more than enough for you, catch the concept that a now word is more than enough. A *revealed* word, a *rhema* word, a *dabar* word, a now *sent* word, an *appointed* word is all you need. Catch that by faith and you will see manifestation over and over and over.

"Send now prosperity." What he was really saying was *"send the word of prosperity."* Send the word. The word *"send"* here and *"sent"* in Psalm 105 are the same Hebrew word meaning sending the word.

Send now a word of prosperity. *"I am not worthy Lord that you come under my roof. But you speak the word only and my servant shall be healed."*[15] You mean a *"word"*? Yes. A fresh word is what it is all about in the kingdom of God. That is how you get everything. That is how

---

[15] Matthew 8:8

everything was created in the first place. The Bible says He upholds all things by the Word of His power.[16] That is how it keeps on functioning.

When we understand that then we enter great faith. The centurion understood it. Jesus said He had not seen so great faith in all of Israel. The centurion amazed the Lord.

God wants us to enter into prosperity. The Hebrew word for *prosperity* means to break out and to break through. To break out of whatever is holding you back and to break through into whatever you are supposed to go into to make you a success. It is not only about money, but money is included. It might mean that you are going to break out of a poverty mentality. You are going to break out of sickness. You are going to break out of bondage. You are going to break through into your destiny. You are going to break through into what you were born to accomplish.

Prosperity covers everything. It means being successful on every level, including financial. It means having a successful marriage, being successful with your family, with relationships. It means being successful in your health. Prosperity means being successful with the dreams that God has given you, with what you were called to do in life. It means that whatever your hand touches starts prospering no matter what you do. It means being successful in your soul winning. It means being successful in outreach ministry to the world. It means being successful in your dream, your vision. That is all prosperity. It covers everything. To break out and to break through.

Do you want to get a prosperity now word, the kind that breaks you out and gets you through? Do you want to know how to position yourself for that? I am going to share some secrets that I believe will help you to tap into the sent word that brings prosperity now, that brings the breakout and the breakthrough, how to get that kind of word from God. We are going to be talking about how to tap into the Spirit and draw out a send now prosperity word.

I have to start by giving you a warning about things that stop this flow from happening. Our next scripture begins by giving a warning

---

[16] Hebrews 1:3

before it gives a blessing. What good is it to hook you up if it is going to be short-circuited?

Psalms 1:1; *"Blessed is the man that walketh not in the counsel of the ungodly, nor standeth in the way of sinners, nor sitteth in the seat of the scornful."*

"...walketh not in the counsel of the ungodly..."

If you want to pull out a *send now* word you can't walk in the counsel of the ungodly. That means you can't be listening to what the world has to say about prosperity. You can't be listening to what the television has to say about prosperity. If you listened to what the world said, you would be so afraid that you would just crawl into a hole and die there. But I am not moved by that. You can't be moved by family, friends, or anyone around you. You can't even be moved by Christians who don't have faith. It would be like taking advice on how to raise your children from someone who never raised kids. Kind of ridiculous isn't it to get your advice about prosperity from someone who knows nothing about it, getting advice about healing from someone who never was healed.

You will be blessed if you don't walk in the counsel of the ungodly. The word *"blessed"* means to have abundance. You will have abundance if you don't listen to bad counsel, including the voice of the devil speaking negativity to you. You can't listen to your own mind for the devil is speaking into it. The mind is the battlefield of satan. *"Oh, I don't listen to the devil."* But you listen to your thoughts all the time and the devil is speaking into your thoughts. The Bible says that a man has to forsake his own thoughts. So, to move on with God you have to forsake your own thoughts and start taking on His thoughts, which is the Word of God. Any thought that is not the Word of God must be held in captivity to the very power of God.[17] Cast down vain imaginations and every high thing that exalted itself against the Name of God. Bring into captivity every thought to the obedience of Christ. Don't walk in the counsel of

---

[17] 2 Corinthians 10:4-5

your own mind. Don't walk in the counsel of your own reasoning because it is diabolically opposed to God. You can't even take your own counsel. You have to take His. You can't trust your own counsel. You have to trust His.

"...nor standeth in the way of sinners..."

When you start listening to ungodly counsel you start blocking sinners from coming to the Gospel. Every time you listen to bad counsel that is not God counsel you become a stumbling block for sinners, they can't get to God through you because you are standing in the way. You are doing the wrong stuff. You got the wrong counsel.

"...nor sitteth in the seat of the scornful..."

I cannot get into a spirit of criticizing, fault finding, being critical, being judgmental, finding the sin in everybody around me and talking about it. All of this will short-circuit what God wants to do in me. I won't get to draw out a send now, prosperity word. I won't get a now word from God. I won't be able to get a sent word, an appointed word from the Lord. I am short-circuiting the whole thing.

We have to get to where we know we have to guard against a critical spirit that finds fault in others and makes us critical of others. Even if they do sin, even if they do fall, that is not our business to get into. It is our business to pray blessing on them and ask God to help them. It is not even our business to get on the phone and tell everybody. *"This is a prayer request, you understand. But I can't believe they fell. I can't believe they did what they did. I tell you what, I can't believe it."* You are short-circuiting anything God can do for you. You are sitting in the seat of the scornful. I am giving you a warning. You have to cast that off, resist it like you resist a rattlesnake. It is just as dangerous and maybe more so. You have to resist that like you would resist a disease or a plague that was coming your way. You and I cannot afford to get into the talking thing where we talk about everybody's problems, everybody who is messing up, every preacher who ever did anything wrong. We get into actually enjoying that mess. We haven't got time for that. It is taking away from what God wants to do in us. I haven't got time for that kind of talk because it will stop what God wants to fulfill in me.

Because this is a warning, if you mess up then repent of it, lay it down and go on. The Bible will tell you what you shouldn't do and it will tell you what you should do.

Psalms 1:2; *"But his delight is in the law of the LORD; and in his law doth he <u>meditate day and night.</u>"*

Don't delight in hearing what other people have to say about things. Don't delight in sitting in the seat of the scornful. If you get to where you enjoy gossip, you need to repent because you are taking on a spirit. You will have to rebuke it out of your life. Don't get to where you enjoy it. Abhor it.

Meditate means to go over and over something in order to apply it to your life. Maybe even speak it to yourself. Go over and over the words until it dawns on you how to apply that scripture to your daily life. That is meditation.

Psalms 1:3; *"And he shall be like a tree planted by the rivers of water, that bringeth forth his fruit in his season; his leaf also shall not wither; and <u>whatsoever he doeth shall prosper.</u>"*

He will be doing what he meditated on. Your life will head the direction of your most predominate thoughts. What you think about the majority of your time is what will be produced in your life. What you meditate on will become mandatory in your life. What you meditate on will begin to be created in your life. Sooner or later it is going to appear in your life or it will happen that your whole life will be transferred to where that situation is. It is either or. Either it will be created or you will be catapulted to where it is. It will manifest. It will either bring it to you or take you to it.

Feed and Seed

3 John 1:2; *"Beloved, I wish above all things that thou mayest prosper and be in health, even as thy soul prospereth."*

How can I enter into prosperity? It is by meditation on the Word of God. Meditation in order to do it. Meditating in order to put it into practice. John said he was going to prosper and be in health as his soul prospered in the knowledge of the Word.

Can you see that this is not all about money? If you have already been obedient in all the other areas of giving, sowing, doing what God tells you to do, you still can't get prosperity without a word from God. Without a sent word you can give all your money away and sit around wondering what is going on. It will not be produced without a word. You have to be renewed to the Word of God or prosperity will never happen for you.

It took me a long time to catch this. But after I had been obedient in giving, sowing and doing everything God told me to do (which is the biggest part of financial prosperity) and prosperity doesn't come, I know what is lacking. I need a sent word. I have to meditate on the scriptures about prosperity and feed on them until a sent word comes.

Joshua needed to become prosperous in his vision. He didn't need money in his situation, but he sure needed to prosper. He needed to break out in order to break through in his ministry of leading the children of Israel. God gave him the formula.

Joshua 1:8; *"This book of the law shall not depart out of thy mouth* [we need to be speaking the Word a lot]*; but thou shalt meditate therein day and night, that thou mayest observe to do according to all that is written therein: for then thou shalt make thy way prosperous, and then thou shalt have good success."*

This verse is talking about staying in the Word day and night until it becomes so alive to you that you begin doing what it says. Then you make your way prosperous by speaking it, by meditating on it and by acting on it until it manifests. How long will that take? It takes until…

TIME

In due season you will reap, if you faint not. When is the due season? Whenever it is due. Sometimes only God knows when it will manifest. The fact is the Word said it would. So all you have to do is keep on keeping on until it does. It is just a matter of time.

Have you heard of seedtime and harvest? Let's not throw them too close together. It is seeding, it is time and then it is harvest. In the middle of sowing a seed and a harvest is a big gap of time. Only God knows how much T I M E is between the sowing of the seed and the reaping of the harvest. Where most people miss it is with the T I M E. They give up before the harvest manifests. But God says that as long as the earth remains there will be seed, time and harvest. The harvest is just as sure as the seeding is, but so is the time. We all have to do our time.

Have you ever noticed that the majority of your life is waiting? Have you lived long enough and been wise enough to observe that most of your life you are waiting for something? We wait for paychecks. We wait for certain things to happen in our lives. We wait in line for things. We wait for the light to turn green. We wait at the grocery store in line, sometimes for a long time. Everything has this waiting thing going on.

But we don't want God to do anything like that at all. We want to give up on Him if He doesn't produce it instantaneously. The Bible says it is through faith and patience that we inherit every promise. If you are willing to hang in there and endure because you know the sent word will always produce something, you will always see the results. You will always get it.

Sinking Roots

Isaiah 37:31; *"And the remnant that is escaped of the house of Judah shall again <u>take root downward, and bear fruit upward</u>:"*

Notice, the Bible speaks about roots that go down deep and bear fruit upward. To bear fruit means success.

We are seeing that you must sink your roots deep into the Word of God in order to draw out what is necessary to produce the fruit. Do you know what the taproot of a tree does? It goes down deep and draws out the nutrients necessary to produce fruit. That is what happens when we begin to meditate, when we begin to go to God, when we begin to fill ourselves with the Word of God. We sink a taproot deep in the Spirit that draws out a sent word which will produce fruit.

Only a sent word, an appointed word will produce fruit. We can't get that superficially. You cannot look at the top of the ground and get it, but have to go down deep into God's Word. You have to sink a taproot deep into God and go down deep so that you can shoot straight up and produce fruit. Go downward in God so you may go upward in success.

This is one of the ingredients to entering into the send now prosperity and actually prospering. There have been times when everything has shut down and I didn't know what I was going to do. There were no revival services, no open door to bring in any finances whatsoever. Yet I had been faithful in tithes and in giving, which is a big part of it. The biggest part of a cake is flour, but flour by itself is not good. You don't have a cake with just flour. But without flour you don't have much of a cake either.

It is the same way with financial prosperity. The biggest part of financial prosperity is your giving, but it won't stand by itself. You still won't prosper. There is an ingredient of the Word that has to come. You have to have a sent word. You have to have a now word. You have to sink a taproot deep into the Word of God that you may be able to shoot up and produce the fruit of prosperity.

Faith

Another part of getting prosperity now is faith. You can't get anything from God without believing. You can't prosper just because you give. You have to believe God. You have to believe that He is a rewarder of those who diligently seek Him. You have to believe that if you sow you are going to reap. You have to believe that if you are obedient to God He will send a tremendous harvest your way. You have to believe it. To not believe it sabotages the whole harvest.

In Mark 9:23 there was a man who came to Jesus. Jesus told him that all things are possible – prosperity is a thing – to him who believes. So, you have to believe to get it. You have to believe God. Faith comes by hearing and hearing by the Word of God. So, if you are not meditating on the Word, you definitely won't have any faith. You must exercise your faith. You must believe God. If you believe God strong enough you will act on His Word as well. You will do what His Word says in order to prosper.

God Is Your Source

Now for another ingredient. Make God your source.

Deuteronomy 8:18; *"But thou shalt remember the LORD thy God: for it is he that giveth thee power to get wealth, that he may establish his covenant which he sware unto thy fathers, as it is this day."*

God simply does not put up with being put on the back burner. He doesn't play second fiddle to anybody. He is either number one, or He is out of there. He said, *"Thou shall have no other gods before me."*

Do you know what people do when they worship a false God? Do they only just pray to that false god? What else do they do? They give offerings. Watch them. They give offerings of money, food, clothes to their gods. They just don't just pray. They give. They sacrifice.

God said, *"There will be no false gods before Me."* He was saying that we have to remember He is the reason we prosper. He is the reason we are blessed. He is the reason we have finances and we need to know that. But we have to make Him our source. Don't make your own ability your source.

I remember one man saying that there was no way he was going to give anything to God. He worked hard for what he got. Then another man told him that if it wasn't for God, he couldn't work. God gives you the strength to work so you can make something. It is not by the might of your own hands. If you get too lifted up on that you could lose the strength of your own arm and not be able to make a dime. So where does it really come from? *"It was the might of my arm. My wisdom did this. I am the one who got out and made it happen."* No, you didn't. If it wasn't for God, you couldn't make anything happen.

We have to come to the place where we understand that the source of all blessing is God. We must make Him our source. Realize that He is and set Him up as the source of everything you need. When you do that it won't matter what happens around you. You are still going to be taken care of. If one door closes and He is your source, you won't worry about it. You know He will open another one. If something happens here it is okay, you know something else is going to take place because God is your source. If God isn't your source and a door closes you are in trouble. You are going to crash. You are going to be upset and your whole world will fall apart. When 9/11 took place there were people who fell even though they didn't die. Why, because the World Trade Center represented the economy. They said that when the stock market crashed many years ago, during the great depression, millionaires jumped out of windows and killed themselves. Why? Because God was not their source. They were their own source. When their little world crashed, everything was over.

My grandpa had a third grade education and little money, but he trusted in God as his source. He always had a job. He always had a vehicle. He always had a house, clothes, money. He raised children during the great depression, fed them and clothed them. No matter what happened, it didn't shake him. God was his source.

In the world we are living in right now, we are going to have to come to the place of not knowing what tomorrow holds, but we do know *Who* holds tomorrow. We need to make God our source for all things including prosperity, the breakthrough and the breakout. You have to make Him the source of it all. If you will, then no matter what happens you will do well. You will be taken care of. You will be blessed. God has to be your source.

Serve God

Another ingredient is found in Exodus 23.

Exodus 23:25-26; *"And ye shall serve the LORD your God, and he shall bless* [give abundance] *thy bread, and thy water; and I will take sickness away from the midst of thee. There shall nothing cast their young, nor be barren, in thy land: the number of thy days I will fulfil."*

If you serve the Lord that means you are not serving yourself or other gods. To serve Him is to live for Him, to obey Him, to do what He says, and to live your whole life just for Him. Are we really serving the Lord? Is our whole life bound up in obeying Him, loving Him, following Him, doing His commandment, pleasing Him? If it is, then you are serving the Lord.

If you serve the Lord, He will take care of you. Serve the Lord and you will never lack anything. My grandpa told me to always serve the Lord. God always took care of him. He always had enough and more. He was even able to help some of the poor folks. He was able to split his groceries with families who didn't have anything. He was able to help people because he had so much in the midst of the depression when there weren't any jobs, there wasn't any food, there wasn't any extra. People with doctorate degrees, training and college educations were out of jobs. They were sitting on the curbs with their families starving. There were no jobs to be had. But God always supplied a job for him. Always supplied finances, a vehicle and a house, food, clothes and whatever they needed.

If you want to enter into the send now prosperity then serve the Lord with all your heart. Give Him your all.

Witty Inventions

This next key is very important. It is entering a time when God starts trusting you with a sent word and a word of instruction that brings witty inventions which produce and draw upon the wealth of the wicked.

We are talking about big stuff. I know some people who have tapped into this.

Proverbs 8:12; *"I wisdom dwell with prudence* [wisely applying knowledge]*, and find out* [discover] *knowledge of witty inventions."*

Wisdom is the Word of God. It is a sent word, a *rhema* word, a *dabar* word, a now word, an appointed word. There is no greater wisdom than God's Word, particularly that which is made alive by the Spirit of God.

Are you ready to discover a sent word that is so creative it changes your life and prospers you beyond your wildest dreams? Are you ready for that? It doesn't matter how qualified you think you are, the Word of God will produce this for you.

This wisdom, this sent word, causes you to find out or discover knowledge of witty inventions. *"Witty"* in Hebrew means expert or intelligent, prosperous inventions. *"Invention"* in Hebrew means the plans, devices, the thoughts. An invention is whatever you need, whether it is a thought, a device, information or the plan that would make you successful in that which God has destined for you. It is not just finances only. It might be how to do a crusade. It might be how to win some people to the Lord. It might be how to fill a church with people. It might be how to pay off a mortgage.

There is a man to whom we had been ministering for over a year. He had been sowing seed, giving offerings. But more than anything God has been changing his mentality from poverty thinking to prosperity thinking. God had me prophesy many times to him about witty inventions. I once asked him if he had a whole book of ideas that God has given him. He answered yes.

In one of the services I had at the church he attends, God told me not to take an offering. It was my first service after a trip to Mexico. I had 700 pesos (about 66 dollars) left when we left Mexico and then God told me to help buy a piano for one of the churches so I handed the money to one of the pastors. When I returned to the States, I had nothing to change back into American money. So, when I returned home I needed finances.

So, I preached that night and God told me not to take an offering. I didn't. It didn't make any sense to my head, but in my heart I knew what the Lord had told me to do. Instead I encouraged the people to pray for us. This man, the one who has been getting the witty inventions, devices and thoughts, walked up to me and said, *"I know you are not taking an offering, but I am giving one. Here is $150. I don't have a lot of money, but God told me to give this amount. I scraped it all together and am putting it in your hand."* This is what this man does every time he sees me. He is becoming a multi, multi-millionaire.

A Key to Prosperity

God spoke to me about a key. In the Spirit there is always a key, whether it is a vision, a device or a plan, but it is one little thing you can do that unlocks everything. The key to every church growing and booming is this prosperous word – send now prosperity. There is a place, through what we are sharing, where you can receive this. Every family needs it to make their home successful. Every marriage needs it to make their marriage successful. Every business, every worker who works somewhere needs it. Every salesperson, every mother, every father needs it. It doesn't matter what you are doing. You need a send now prosperity word. What I am sharing everyone of us can latch on to.

A sent word will fill the church and reach the lost. Every church has a different key. Each church, every pastor needs to seek God for a send now word that will break that thing loose just for them. You can't use somebody else's word. This has to come alive to you.

Several years ago I was seeking the Lord for direction because I didn't know what I was going to do. I was meditating, feeding and seeding. Up bubbled a word and this word brought vision. The vision brought blessing. It was the scripture, *"Daily I load you down with benefits."*[18] A send now word, I started meditating on it.

I had spent a lot of time in the Word just going over prosperity scriptures until this surfaced. Then as I meditated on it every day, God gave me an inner vision of people knocking on my door giving me money.

---

[18] Psalm 68:19

The vision was connected to the Word. Once I had that, I had peace. My wife asked me what we were going to do. I told her it was all right. I had heard from God and I told her the vision. She said that had to be God because no one had ever come to our door and handed us money before.

The send now word brings vision. 1 Samuel 3 says that the Word of the Lord was precious. That means it was scarce. There was no open vision. Without a vision people perish. It starts with a now word. You have to first have a now word which will produce a vision. When the vision comes what you see you be. What you perceive, you receive.

Three days later it started happening. People were knocking on our door giving us money. Seven hundred dollars started flowing to my door every week for the period I was not preaching. When I started preaching revivals again, it quit happening. It is kind of like the manna in the wilderness. When the Israelites got over into the kingdom land it quit. God provides one way or another as long as you have a sent word.

It changes our view of things. Now I am not afraid to give because either I have a sent now word or I will get one. Your liberal giving can bring a send now word. Your liberality and faith in God can bring a send now word from heaven. Your lack of obedience to God can stop a send now word. One send now word can bring a prosperous plan, a prosperous device, an idea, a thought that will change your life forever. It only takes one.

Prosperity is not what you have on the outside. It is what you have on the inside. I talked to a man who is a millionaire many times over. He said he could always get millions. Any time he lost it, he knew how to go back and get it again. He did not have to have a million dollars to get another million.

Prosperity is not what you have in your hand. It is what you are on the inside. If you have a poor self-image on the inside, you will be poor. If you have that kind of self-image, you will have to change it with the Word by putting the Word inside you. The Word will give you a good self-image. You will be able to see yourself as prosperous. *"Why, I could never see myself like that."* If you can't see yourself as prosperous you will never be that way. *"I tell you, I don't believe I will ever have millions."* You won't.

I will and I will tell you why. First, I am going to do the word. Second, when I get it, God has plans to use it for the Gospel. I am going to be able to go to all different countries because I am going to be prosperous enough to afford it. I am going to be able to build churches all around the world. I am going to be prosperous enough to do it.

One lady is praying for a jet airplane for me. She said God showed her I needed a jet airplane and she is standing in faith with me until I get it. She said I would be so busy that I would need it. I told her okay, I would agree with her if she would help me birth it. She agreed. That takes millions of dollars. I don't have to have millions of dollars. All I have to have is a send now prosperity word and that send now prosperity word will produce it. God can give me one little idea that is so simple it is ridiculous to the natural mind. Everyone will think it has already been done. I won't have to sell it or hardly do anything with it. Write it on paper and send it off with a stamp. Then just sit back, enjoy what comes in and do what I need to do with the rest of it. *"I just can't see it."* Then you won't be it.

Everyone needs this to do what God has called you to do. God has given some a vision so big that it takes God to do it. You will have to get a send now word in order to be able to accomplish it. If I can preach this so you believe it, I can help you get into a new day in the spirit.

God can give you one little idea. He can tell you what to do. He can show you how to do this and how to do that. We are going to see the wealth of the wicked transferred and most of it will come with a business idea or an invention, not just sitting back doing nothing. Most of it will not come by you winning the lottery. It will come with a business idea, an invention or with something God tells you to do. You have to have a sent word from heaven.

Made in the USA
Columbia, SC
07 October 2020